WILL MRS. MAJOR GO TO HELL?

Contents

CONTENTS

WILL MRS. MAJOR GO TO HELL?

Introduction

For years I've been retelling one of Aloïse Buckley Heath's autobiographical stories to disgruntled dinner guests. It had to do with an encyclopedia she bought on the installment plan; her haphazard way of paying for it; the computerized collection agency which, when she missed a month, mistakenly sent her the seventh instead of the first in a series of nine nasty letters; the riotous escalation of threats and reprisals; and the final attempt by the encyclopedia to garnishee her husband's salary at the oil company where he worked.

The encyclopedia was informed that Mrs. Heath owned a tenth of the oil company and that the other nine-tenths were owned by her nine brothers and sisters.

As I told the story, I could see each sentence in my mind. In comes this delightful collection of her articles. Eagerly, I sought the original. It wasn't there. Why wasn't it there? Because she had never gotten around to putting it down on paper. She was, as Priscilla Buckley (a sister) and William F. Buckley Jr. (a brother) note, "notoriously disorganized . . . she would agree to write anything in the world any editor asked her to write; and simply did not do so."

One reason why she didn't do so is that she was the mother of ten children. Her family came first. And it was her family, the ones she grew up with and the ones she helped to grow up, that she usually wrote about. An extraordinary crew, reminding one (if they will permit an invidious analogy) of the Kennedys: the Roman Catholicism, the patriarch, the family compound, the loyalty, wit, charm, industry, and tragedy. Indeed, it seems almost as though the Buckleys and the Kennedys were engaged in a war of propagation to determine who will inherit the earth.

Whether she's describing the childhood of her famous brother (at age six, Bill B. wrote the King of England demanding he pay back the war debt); or solving the Santa Claus problem ("Sweetie, how should I know why Polly's Santa Claus is really her father? Maybe her father *has* to be her Santa Claus, poor little thing! Maybe Santa Claus just doesn't *like* Polly. Did you ever think of that?"); or exploring the sociology of the carpool ("without carpools, private schools would cease to exist; public schools would be in a state of pandemonium, what with having to take in all those private-school children; and this nation would have to appraise candidly the possibility of the Central Congolese getting to Mars before us")—she is graceful, witty, opinionated, memorable.

Take a for-instance: "The average man is well into his twenties before he is able to get angry without trying to fight; and he is well into the next world before he stops losing his temper, shouting, slamming doors, swearing. Twice as many men as women have nervous breakdowns, three times as many commit suicide, four times as many have ulcers, and there are fifty times more unpremeditated attacks and a hundred times more unpremeditated murders by men than by women. But you know what women do, don't you? Women *cry*! Women cry because women are more emotional than men, that's why."

Or her attempt to re-create a love scene in a ladies' magazine "in the course of which a woman stood 'with her hands clasped on Loren's neck, her red hair pressed against his chin, her lips ardently uplifted.' The trouble is, when *I* clasp *my* hands on my husband's neck, press *my* interestingly graying hair against his chin, and ardently uplift *my* lips, all *I* get is a mouthful of Adam's apple."

Or her hilarious grappling with the new math in an article called "Spare Me the Rods," ending with the realization that on a single morning a kindergarten class was "brought to see the logic of doubleness and halfness, which is a pretty big thing to understand. . . . I wondered, too, if the New Mathematics, or the modern mathematics, is not simply the mathematical application of a very old science called logic; and whether the 'new' techniques are not as old as Socrates, helping the young men of Athens nearly twenty-five hundred years ago to stumble their wordy way toward eternal verities."

Best of all are Mrs. Heath's annual Christmas reports, her attempts to imitate the Trapp family, to tape her children's caroling ("'Just who,' I asked, in my most restrained voice, 'is Round John Virgin?' 'One of the twelve opossums,' the ten young voices answered promptly, and they collapsed over the piano"), to instruct her brood on the meaning of the world. It was on Christmas Eve, 1967, that she collapsed, and two weeks later died, at age forty-eight.

Those readers who must spray a sort of ideological antiseptic over every book before sitting down to grapple with it should be warned right now that Mrs. Heath had what some would say were unfashionable political opinions, like the rest of her family, and they are to be found in this book. She voted for Goldwater, she made fun of the U.N. Declaration of the Rights of Children, she opposed Khrushchev's visit to the United States, and she was one of the most successful fund-raisers in Smith College history when she proposed to her fellow alumnae that they withhold their contributions until the college explained the affiliations of several professors.

If that puts anyone off from reading this book, the anyone is indeed impoverished. I remember a story she never finished writing; and although I never met her, I feel I know her now on the basis of her book, and am the richer for the acquaintance. After that last sad Christmas, her youngest child said: "Nothing will ever be fun again."

John Leonard

New York Times
July 17, 1969

CHAPTER I

Supper at Great Elm

Great Elm was the Buckley's sprawling home in the Berkshire Hills in Sharon, Connecticut, one hundred miles north of New York City where Will Buckley, who was in the oil business and away from home for long stretches of time, kept an apartment. Aloïse Buckley and the children—seven of them in 1928—spent the summers at Great Elm, assisted by Mademoiselle Bouchex, the French governess in charge of the four eldest, and by two Mexican nurses, Josefina and Felipa, who took care of the little ones. The children were Aloïse, 9; John, 7; Priscilla, 6; Jimmy, 5; Jane, 3; Billy, 2; Patricia, a few months old. Papa came home on weekends, and that's when the fun began.

The years when Father was still Papa seem, through the haze of twenty and thirty years, to consist only and forever of family supper in the shadowed summer twilight of the big dining-room at Great Elm. Dinner must have been early on those evenings, for in memory, the sun glints strongly through the heavy elms beyond the western windows, and a curtain is always being drawn, or a blind lowered in order to present a child with a clearer and more comfortable view of his unfinished tuna fish on toast. There are no guests on these occasions, which is the reason Aloïse and John and Priscilla and Jimmy and Mademoiselle are having dinner in the upper-dining-room with Mama and Papa. Jane, Billy, and Patricia, too young to be so honored,

13

are at their own table in the lower-dining-room, happily not eating their vegetables, because Mexican Nana, *their* supervisor, has her meals in the kitchen. Reid, Maureen, and Carol are placidly unborn.

One of the delicious distinctions of dinner in the upper-dining-room is that you have to speak English because it is not polite to speak French in front of Papa, whose other language is only Spanish, poor thing. Sometimes, though, Mademoiselle, who is absent-minded, relapses into middle-dining-room *mores* and says: "Parlez français, s'il-vous-plait," which is very amusing indeed. But sometimes Jane or Billy calls: "Papá! Papá!"—they, who speak only Spanish and a little French, aren't even *trying* to learn English!—and the big children try to wring from a reluctant Mademoiselle the admission that if it is "pas poli" for them to speak French in the presence of Papa, it is equally "pas poli" for Papa to speak Spanish in *her* presence. Mama is neutral: she speaks inaccurate French and Spanish with great fluency and nonchalance and she has told us that what Papa says about how she must practice her mistakes, making so many of them, is not true; they just come naturally when she opens her mouth.

Mother sits at the pantry, or "bell-end" of the table—("Just your Mother's polite way of putting it. She's afraid if she admits it's the head of the table, you children will realize she's the head of the family," and "Oh, *Papa!*" the children giggle, thrilled by the outrageousness of his invention). Aloïse sits next to Mama, because Aloïse is both plain and argumentative and Papa, often articulately, deplores these characteristics in any female of any age. Jimmy is in the chair on Mama's other side because Jimmy (a) makes smacking noises when he chews, (b) never gets the backs of his hands clean, (c) chatters incessantly in a physically unbearable penny-whistle screech, and Papa, often articulately, deplores these characteristics in any person of any age. (Another reason Jimmy sits beside Mama is that (d) Jimmy and Mama are each other's favorite.) John and Priscilla sit in secure serenity on either side of Papa because they are by nature clean and pretty, sweet-tempered and mellow, and can therefore only be teased about things they don't mind. Mademoiselle's place is between Priscilla and Jimmy because they are very young, still, and in more need than the others of the little, murmured "Pas avec les mains," and "Finissez vos legumes, s'il-vous-plait," and "Ne parlez *pas* avec la bouche *pleine*, Zhee-mee! (Jimmy)" with which she punctuates all meals in the upper-dining-room.

At the foot of the table sits Papa, eating, talking, laughing, teasing, dominating the table with the gusto and vigor, the gaiety and the concentration on the moment at hand which, until his last illness, entered the house and left it only with him. (Only when he turns to Mademoiselle does his manner change to the grave and slightly puzzled courtesy with which he treats all plain women: "Father's 'What *can* God have been thinking of?' expression," his daughters called it, many years later.)

Papa is the biggest man in the world and the smartest. He can lasso children by the leg while they're running. He is the strongest man in the world but also the kindest, which keeps him from beating up other children's Papas. He has the bluest eyes and the pinkest cheeks in the world and he is 99 years old. (Mama is 16.) He is the handsomest man in the world, and aside from the King of England, the richest: he owns personally ONE HUNDRED DOLLARS. He has never told a lie in his entire life except for jokes and kneels by his bed every morning to say his prayers. God will, naturally, send him straight to Heaven when he dies, except for perhaps an hour or so in Purgatory so as not to show favoritism. He is the most modest man in the world, because he says none of these things are true; that Mama made them up to show what good taste she had when she proposed to him. He is the funniest man in the world.

Papa is George Washington and Douglas Fairbanks, Will Rogers and Robin Hood, King Arthur and Stonewall Jackson. Mama thinks so, too (and thought so, to the day of his death), although as her children, growing up, began to come to her with stories of how absolutely *impossible* Father was getting to be, she used to confuse them into silence by retorting that: (a) they could count themselves lucky if they ever again, in the course of their lives, laid *eyes* on a man of their father's caliber, and (b) they were all beginning to exaggerate just like their father.

At supper in the summertime, Papa talks to the children about the olden days when he was young, and these are the things he tells them:

—His father's name was John, and John was so strong that when he was only 17 years old he used to go to country fairs without telling his parents, and win ten dollars by beating the wrestler. It was no wonder, therefore, that when he grew up he became a TEXAS SHERIFF. Unfortunately, he never shot any- one, but then, on the other hand, no one ever shot him—a circumstance from which the children are supposed to derive more comfort than they, in fact, do. He once let Papa ride all the way to Kansas City with him in a cattle car, even though Papa's mother thought he was too little.

—His mother's name was Mary Ann, not Mother B., as the children had always supposed. She was very beautiful and very good but very strict, and though Papa was born on July 12th, she celebrated his birthday on July 11th because July 12th is Orangeman's Day. (Father's 77th and last birthday was cele- brated, as always, on July 11th.) When she saw Grandfather talking and laughing with a man who didn't like him, and whom he didn't like, she would say later: "John, how *can* you!" She would say: "I can forgive by an act of *my* will, but can only forget by an act of God's will." And Papa, telling this, rocks back in his chair, mouth opened wide in one of his great bursts of laughter. "You kno-o-w?" he says, "I don't remember God's ever willing my mother to forget a single thing she willed herself to forgive!" (Yet when Aloïse once asked, all big-eyed and fraudulent innocence, if Mother B. would have shot people if *she* had been the Texas Sheriff, Father lost his good humor at once and answered shortly: "That will do, Aloïse. My mother was a saint, and don't any of you ever forget it." Thus early do the children learn, as their own children and husbands and wives have since learned, that Buckleys tolerate disparagement of Buckleys only from Buckleys—and only from Buckleys within the same degree of consanguinity, at that.)

—There was Uncle John, who was the oldest, and who died when he was 16 (and in such a way as to at least mitigate the callous and unromantic pacifism of the children's grandfather, for he died of pneumonia after he was waylaid and stabbed in the lung by a boy who believed he had been the victim of an unfair decision in a baseball match John had refereed); and there was Tía (Aunt) Priscilla, and Papa, who was Willie then, and Uncle Claude and Tía Eleanor and Uncle Edmund, who was the baby. (It seems strange to the children, when they are very small, that the next-to-youngest should have the whitest hair, but by the time they are ten or so, it has become evident that Tía Eleanor's hair was a good forty years older than Tía Eleanor.) John and Priscilla and Claude and Eleanor and Edmund were all paragons of intelligence, wit, honor, diligence, piety, courage, CHARACTER (Papa's capitals), and any other virtue you could think of. They were all far superior to Papa, he says, and if Mama had not already explained that all the Buckleys were additionally gifted with the quality of modesty, the children might have pitied their poor, inferior Papa.

—Uncle Claude had a terrible temper when he was small, but when he got old, when he was 19, he lost the handball doubles championship of the University of Texas because he insisted on having Papa as his partner, so the children forgive him the fact that he once hit Papa on the nose with a brick and broke it, which is why his nose is so big and curved. ("Big and crooked," says Papa. "Aristocratic," says Mama.) "Your Father must be getting very vain in his old age if he's taken to inventing wild tales to explain the Buckley nose," says Tía Priscilla, whose nose is small and straight. "Your Aunt would rather face my terrible nose than your Uncle Claude's terrible temper," says Papa. Uncle Claude smiles and shakes his head and winks at the children, which is what Uncle Claude mostly does. The issue is, to this day, unresolved.

—When Papa was a little boy, he used to creep out of the house at four o'clock in the morning and run down to the town jail to share the prisoners' breakfast of doughnuts and *café con leche*. The jailer allowed him this privilege because his father was the sheriff; the coffee, perhaps because it was served with milk, fortunately did not stunt his growth, though it will stunt the children's growth if they drink it before they are 16. (Once, when John asked Papa something about those early breakfasts, he said, "*café con leche* with milk in it." Papa laughed at him—very rudely, the children thought; after all, John's language was *French*—and, calling down to the lower-dining-room, explained the joke to the little children, whose unduly prolonged and insufferably Spanish-y giggles were ignored by their seniors, who sat in silence coldly hating Papa. As was truly meet and just, John beat up Jane, Billy, and Patricia right after supper, but Papa, who was supposed to be strolling in the garden, unfairly walked into the nursery during the height of the fracas and sent John to bed with harsh language—which is why John got the .22 he'd been promised only when he was 12, four years early. (Twenty-five years later, one of the young men in the Company remarked to a group of the younger Buckleys that his personal retirement-old age insurance plan was to "make Mr. Buckley fire me . . . First, of course, I have to figure out how to make him mad enough to fire me with a really *big* pension." Mr. Buckley's children agreed that the plan had every chance of success.)

—Papa's school had only one room and only one teacher. The teacher was a man and he had a red beard, but he was a very good teacher nevertheless. When someone had dirty fingernails, he would say: "Are you in mourning?" When someone said "*pre*spiration," he would say: "If you can't say *perspiration*, say 'sweat.'" When someone talked about the "kids," he would say: "In my school there are no young goats." And he would say: "In my school, however little you learn, you will learn to express correctly," so every morning they had a grammar drill on sentences like: "Each of the stories told by the three men were amusing," or "While ill in the hospital, my house burned down." He would say: "In my school you will use words *accurately*" when he heard a big boy swear, and he would make the boy write three sentences on the board using the word "damn" or "God" or "hell" accurately. He would say, "'Gosh' and 'heck' and 'darn' are cowards' swearwords." Papa learned what he was taught, and he remembered and told the children. (Many years later, one of his daughters heard her father say quietly into a telephone: "Mr. X, as far as I'm concerned, you can go right straight to hell," and, smiling to herself, thought of the redbearded teacher in the little Texas town. It was obvious that Papa was expressing himself *correctly* and using his words *accurately*.)

—When Papa was still young, poor grandfather died one night, after a stroke, surrounded by his family. When he died, he didn't have enough money in the bank for Papa and the family to finish school, so for a while Papa became a schoolteacher himself. He had a little school on the Mexican border, where he taught all eight grades, in Spanish mostly, because practically all the children were Mexican. The school was a day and a night away from home, by train or horseback, so from fall to Christmas, and Christmas to Easter, and Easter to summer, Papa boarded at a nearby ranch. Once, in January, when there was a long cold-spell, he pulled back his covers at bedtime and found a rattlesnake coiled between his sheets. Unfortunately, Papa did not know about putting the pan of warm milk on the floor, like Kipling, so he called the rancher's wife (after all, it wasn't *his* house, or *his* bed, or *his* rattlesnake, the children would explain to each other later), and she swept the snake onto the floor with one end of her broom and killed it with the other. "And did she say: 'Tsk, tsk, them pesky critters'?" one of the children, who were all in the age of conformity, would ask. "Of course," Papa would answer gravely. "Then why are you winking at Mama?"

—It took over three years (half a lifetime, if you were Jimmy's age) for Papa to get to be twenty years old and by that time, as might be expected, he had accumulated vast hoards of money not even counting the money that Tía Priscilla gave him from what she earned translating Spanish and English in an Office; so at last Papa could go to the University. (The children know *what* University: *the* University, that's what University.) But even at that University, even though Papa was a schoolteacher, and even though he was twenty years old, they made him take examinations to get in. When he passed those, they made him take freshman final exams in *Spanish*! Then they made him take the sophomore finals and then the junior ("Weren't you *tired*, Papa?" asks the sympathetic Priscilla), and finally the examination that seniors had to take before they graduated with a degree in Spanish. After all that, the University told Papa that he could be in the freshman class, but had to take English and History with the sophomore class and be an Instructor in Spanish, which turned out all right, because every month the University paid him 28 dollars and 50 cents for instructing. ("Lucky *duck!*" the children murmur, wide-eyed and proud.)

—These are the things Papa told the children about his bright college years:

They were among the happiest years of his life.

The first year was lonely, because he lived in a freshman dormitory, where the other boys were 17 and 18, and Papa was twenty and an Instructor.

After his freshman year, he lived in an off-campus house with students from all four classes, and he was happy.

He never saw a football or a baseball game away from the University, because he never had enough money to buy a train ticket, but he often saw home games.

He ate at a restaurant in Austin where you could buy a meal of pea soup, steak, fried potatoes, bread and butter, apple pie, and coffee for 25 cents. ("Yum *yum*," Jimmy murmurs, late on the cue only because he is busy trying to find out how much asparagus hollandaise can be safely hidden beneath a lamb chop bone.)

He and Uncle Claude once convinced a freshman whose final report card was studded with A's that he had flunked out of college because E stood for "Excellent," D for "Doing Well," C for "Can Do Better," B for "Bad," and A for "Awful." "The thing *is*," the children point out to one another in the insomniac hour between summer bedtime and summer sleep, "Papa and Uncle Claude could say it, all right, but the thing *is*, how could they think that freshman really believed it?" The thing *was*, the children were to learn, that Papa, at least, most certainly did think the freshman believed it, for he never entertained the slightest doubt of the success of his practical jokes, which tended to be elaborate and transparent. "She pretended she'd known all along, but you should have seen her blush," he would say about one of his "victims," who had indeed known all along; or, "He tried to laugh the whole thing off, but I could see by the look in his eyes . . . " "Don't tell *me* you didn't think that house was haunted! You were all as white as sheets," he would delightedly inform the children, who protested that they had instantly recognized the paternal "wo-oo-oo-oo's" emanating from the cellar of the empty house next door. Then there was the yearly irritation of Christmas. *All*

the children were firm believers in Santa Claus, Papa maintained, in the teeth of impassioned statements to the contrary;
in spite of Jimmy's pointing out, Christmas after Christmas,
that although Santa Claus experienced no difficulty in convers-
ing in English with half the household, in Spanish with the
other half, he always answered Mademoiselle's "Joyeux Noël,
Sawhnta Close" with a courteously formal: "Thank you,
Mademoiselle. Merry Christmas to you, too." (In their young
adulthood, the children decided that just as the dignity and
reserve which Father kept between himself and all the world
except for very young children demanded occasional release in
the form of practical jokes, so that same dignity and reserve
demanded that these jokes be uniformly successful. In middle-
aged adulthood, the children have not changed their minds.)

One year at the University, when Papa was worried about
not having enough money, he heard of a hundred-dollar prize
that an insurance company would give to whoever wrote the
best composition about some kind of insurance, so he read
about that kind of insurance and wrote the composition and
won the prize. The next year he was worried again about not
having enough money. But because he had won once, he wasn't
allowed to try again, so one of his friends agreed to sign his
name to Papa's essay for ten dollars, so he won the prize again,
though this year it was about a different kind of insurance.
The next year, though, he didn't write the composition, because
he didn't think he could bear to learn any more about insurance.

In the summer vacations, Papa and Uncle Claude and Uncle
Edmund—or was Uncle Edmund too young? Was it Dr. Garnett?—went to Mexico and earned money and had adventures.
One summer they traveled from village to village showing
movies, which they were not very good at doing. However,
the audience didn't mind much when the reels were in the
wrong order, or when they got parts of some movies mixed up
with parts of others, but they did mind very much when Papa

couldn't seem to keep from showing the film upside down ("C'est assez!" Mademoiselle whispers sharply, as the children catch each other's eyes across the table, for it is well and disrespectfully known that, for Papa, locks do not respond to keys, nor corks to corkscrews, nor cars to starters), so after a while the boys decided that Papa could only take turns between being the usher and the ticket taker, but never the movie man. Papa said that was fair. Another time they sold soap that they made every night. It was wonderful soap; the boys used to ask for something very dirty to wash, and after they had washed it, it was all clean and bright again and the people in the villages were very pleased. By the middle of the summer they had sold so much soap that they didn't have anything left to make it with and they had loads of money so they decided they might as well go home. The way home was through some of the same villages they had sold soap to, and at the very first one, all of the women came running out of their houses, screaming and scolding and calling the boys "*ladrones*"—("Robbers," Jimmy translates squeakily, for Jimmy has only very recently been promoted from Nana and the nursery, and sometimes forgets that he is pretending not to know Spanish)—and the women held up the clothes they had washed. The clothes were still clean and bright but ("How can Papa and Mama and Mademoiselle *laugh*?" Aloïse and John, who know the tragic last act, wonder) they were full of big ragged holes. So Papa and Uncle Claude and Uncle Edmund—or was it Dr. Garnett?—paid them back the money they had spent for the soap and gave them money for new clothes and "we got home with 16 cents between the three of us," Papa finishes, simply roaring with laughter. "But they didn't *have* to buy the soap," argues Priscilla in the ensuing pause. (Priscilla is always tiresomely living up to the reputation she established at the age of three, when she answered Aloïse's unflattering comments on a group of Japanese by sweetly lisping: "Maybe *they* think *we* has funny faces, *too!* "—or that's what Mama says she said.) "No-o-o," Papa agrees, thoughtful and instantly intent, "nobody made them buy the soap. They bought the soap because they trusted the three American boys who told them it was good soap." Papa glances round the table once, then begins to eat his lemon pie. The children look triumphantly, but not unsympathetically at Priscilla. After all, you can't always guess right.

And then . . . and then . . . But the stories of when Papa lived in Mexico, the days when he was a lawyer and when he was an oil man and when he was in revolutions and when he met Mama must wait, for the candles have flickered down and the sun has set. It is almost time for baths and prayers and bed.

Soon—too soon, it seems today—Papa has turned into Father, and the big children are sons and daughters whose eyes no longer widen as they listen. It is only the smaller children who still have Papa, and to them the stories are told.

Chapter 2

Mademoiselle

"Mademoiselle," more formally known as Jeanne Bouchex, was born at Evian-les-Bains in 1882, and came to us in 1922. She was originally to be Aloïse's governess, but by 1932 John, Priscilla, and Jimmy had also been slipped in on her.

All of us, however, were more or less brought up on one or another of Mademoiselle's *systèmes*. All of us, between the ages of five and 15, have been entered in one of Mademoiselle's innumerable *petits carnets*, in which our daily behavior was characterized by black, blue, or red marks which were summed up every Saturday, to the confusion of all concerned, by black, red, or gold stars. No child, however, ever failed to get a gold star at the end of the week, just as no child ever failed to get an "A" in Mademoiselle's French class. The *petits carnets* were always smudged by her attempts to erase the black marks she had hot-headedly entered for such offenses as sprinkling corn flakes in the cook's bed, departing for parts unknown with Shetland ponies and without permission, or throwing Priscilla off the topmost beam in the hay-loft to test the depth, texture, and general resiliency of the hay. These delinquencies, Mademoiselle, upon mature consideration, always attributed to youthful high spirits; the black marks were erased to make way for the shining star of virtue.

Towards life—or towards us, because we were her life—Mademoiselle's attitude was the same. Although her perceptions were acute and her judgment keen, she never applied either to us. To the problems and perplexities of childhood and maturity; to broken dolls and marital quarrels, algebra failures and love affairs she opened her boundless store of understanding and sympathy and love. She often told each separate child that he had *une petite place spéciale dans mon coeur*. She alone knew how often we used it.

In her little room at Kamschatka, surrounded by the photographs of the children she loved, Mademoiselle died on April 29th, 1949, at ten o'clock in the morning. She left us a living memory and an abiding sense of loss. She took with her the hearts of our childhood, our deep and everlasting love, and the sure knowledge that when she left us she was at peace with herself, her world, and her God.

CHAPTER 3

Memorandum to:

Aloïse (1918)	Billy (1925)
John (1920)	Patricia (1927)
Priscilla (1921)	Reid (1930)
Jimmy (1923)	Maureen (1933)
Jane (1924)	Carol (1938)

W*hile the search for oil kept WFB on the road a great deal of the time, in Venezuela, in Europe, across the States, he was far from being an absentee father to his ten children, and evolved, over the years, a method of communicating his thoughts to them—by Memoranda, whose seriousness of purpose was more often than not subverted by a bracing lacing of parental humor. "Memorandum to:" by Aloïse Heath, WFB's eldest child, was written for* W. F. B.: An Appreciation, *a book the family brought out in 1959, the year after William Buckley's death.*

There was nothing complicated about Father's theory of child-rearing: he brought up his sons and daughters with the quite simple objective that they become absolutely perfect. To this end his children were, at one time or another, given professional instruction in: apologetics, art, ballroom dancing, banjo, bird-watching, building boats in bottles, calligraphy, canoeing, carpentry, cooking, driving trotting horses, French, folk-dancing, golf, guitar (Hawaiian and Spanish), harmony, herb-gardening, history of architecture, horsemanship, ice-skating, mandolin, marimba, music appreciation, organ, painting, piano, playing popular music, rumba, sailing, skiing, singing, Spanish, speech, stenography, swimming, tap-dancing, tennis, typing, and woodcarving.

And from a random culling of the old filing cabinets (until lately stored in the unused part of the chicken coop at Great Elm) it appears that there was very little in the human personality, or in the personalities of Aloïse et al., which he considered unworthy of his attention.

Protruding teeth and romances; poor diction and sophomore marks at college; quarreling, careers, and the choice of a fraternity, were all subjects to which he gave time and thought; about which letters and memoranda—often from a hotel in Caracas, a sleeping car in Spain, an apartment in Paris, or a rented room in London—arrived in due course in college letter box or on Great Elm breakfast table.

The more ephemeral fields of perfectibility he took over himself and (since, from their adolescence on, he and his children were on terms of affectionate inarticulateness) were conducted by means of letters and memoranda, usually signed "Father." Every memorandum was, as a matter of principle, directed to all "the children," so as to conceal from those for whose benefit it was intended the fact that it was they upon whom Father's eye was fixed. In March 1956, for instance, 16-year-old Carol received at boarding-school a letter informing her that:

Your Mother and I feel very strongly that your children should have at least two injections of the new polio vaccine by June 1 at the latest. This is a matter of such importance that I am sure you realize that any procrastination on your part may result in the death or a life of total paralysis for one or several of your children.

I am informed that these injections are relatively painless and can be given to children as young as two months of age.

Carol, realizing that Father would have considered it indelicate to the point of rudeness to address these instructions *only* to those of his grandchildren's parents whom he knew to be procrastinators, was only momentarily startled. In the interests of common courtesy the memo was, as usual, headed "To the Buckley Children" and followed by "cc: Aloïse, John, Priscilla, Jimmy, Jane, Billy, Patricia, Reid, Maureen, Carol."

Often, however, he addressed his children as a unit, as members of a family which he hoped and planned should become and remain a family or a clan in a very concrete sense. Thus, in 1949, he wrote his children:

I have just read *Prairie Avenue*, by Arthur Meeker, an impressive novel about wealthy families in Chicago during the golden period of 1885 to 1918. These people were pure materialists, without morals or religion, although uniformly contributing members of churches. Notwithstanding their conviction that they were establishing families that would last forever, these had disintegrated entirely by 1918. The following are the appropriate forewords to the three books and epilogue of the novel:

Book I—"The sunny street that holds the gifted few . . . "
                                                          Old Chicago Saying
Book II—"This is the rejoicing city that dwelt carelessly, and said in her heart, I am, and there is none beside me." (*Zephaniah 2:15*)

Book III—"Their inward thought is, that their houses shall continue forever, and their dwelling places to all generations . . . Nevertheless . . . man that is in honour, and understandeth not, is like the beasts that perish."   (*Psalm 48*)

Epilogue: "For he remembered that they were but flesh; a wind that passeth away, and cometh not again."   (*Psalm 79*)

Affectionately,
Father

This seemed unduly critical in view of the fact that Father had just circulated another

MEMORANDUM TO THE CHILDREN:

As you probably know, Americans are famous for being the poorest conversationalists in the world. Education and cultivation of the mind do not seem to improve us. We can't stay on a subject and we are constitutionally incapable of listening. As a people we are always thinking of something we are going to tell the "bore" as soon as he stops talking. A political conversation is never a "give and take," but leads to a monologue—usually by the least interesting and least informed person present.

I am enclosing an article from December's *Reader's Digest*, which you should all read again and again. It is the best thing I have ever seen written on this subject.

Father

and none of the children was quite sure to which it was *really* addressed. Needless to say, the end generation made it a point to be intelligently mute, or mutely intelligent, for a good two weeks.

On one occasion, Father, who considered smoking a sin just this side of adultery, or dirty talk, was irritated to the point of addressing only the guilty. In one of the very few memoranda addressed not to "The children" but to individuals called Aloïse, John, Jane, Billy, Patricia, Reid, he offers the passing comment that:

Knowing your catholic interests in literature, I am quoting from a life of Columbus which recently appeared. Rodrigo, one of Columbus's associates, landed in San Salvador, and made the following quaint statement:

"They pressed lighted tobacco upon us, and Luis de Torres and I, being Andalusians and nothing daunted, inhaled the smoke and straightway were seized into a spasm of coughing and into a dizziness that lightened our heads and mellowed our humors and then to vomiting. Surely this weed was a drug and all the natives used it and perchance that accounted for their debility, for, indeed, they were a fragile people; seemingly not ill and yet never robust."

Father

This preoccupation with the collective character of his children did not, however, deter Father from coming down to earth, if earth needed to be come down to. "My dear John," he wrote, just before John's 14th birthday:

On Sunday you told me that you would see Mr. Tuttle Monday and would write me that day the name of a book on saddle horses. You did not do this Monday, Tuesday, or Wednesday.

My getting a letter from you about this matter is not of great importance, but it is very important that you do what you promised to do. I have noticed invariably that those of my friends who keep their slightest promise are successful and those who don't keep their small promises are not successful.

This is a very slovenly habit to get into and one which promises to be a lifelong habit with you and Aloïse if you don't correct it right away. After this, when I ask you to do anything I wish you would think it over seriously and if you decide it is too much trouble tell me then that you won't do it. I quite understand that your training in doing things has been very deficient, but you and Aloïse are now old enough to do some thinking for yourself and develop your own character.

Affectionately,
Father

cc to Miss Aloïse Buckley

Again to Jim, aged 16:

Mr. James Buckley
Millbrook School
Millbrook, New York

My dear Jimmy:
I am returning to you my check for $10.00, and am sending you an additional check for $24.00. The $34.00 is a return of money you paid me to reimburse me for the purchase of the binoculars, which I am giving you as a present. Your Mother and I remarked Sunday afternoon that we were very pleased at the seriousness with which

you take your debts. She said you had paid her everything you owed her.

With lots of love,

Affectionately,
Father

On another occasion, Father wrote the headmistress of the Ethel Walker School:

I have intended for some time to write or speak to you about Maureen's speech. She does not speak distinctly and has a tendency, in beginning a sentence, to utter any number of words almost simultaneously. Anything that the school may do to improve this condition would be greatly appreciated by us. I have always had a feeling that there was some physical obstruction that caused this, but doctors say there is not. She is one of two or three children in our family who have no wisdom teeth—perhaps this has something to do with it. I hope you will pardon my adding to your many burdens.

He did not circulate, beyond the eldest five children, his description of the night when, in Mother's absence, Father and eight-year-old Maureen were roommates:

After Maureen and I had played two games of Parchesi and I had read her one story and she had read me one story, I mentioned the fact that it was almost two hours past her bedtime. Your sister asked me pointedly where her Mother and I habitually undressed for bed. I replied that your Mother usually undressed in the bathroom while I read the evening paper, and when your Mother had come to bed, I took my turn in the bathroom. I added that, in view of her superior sex, Maureen would be given priority in the bathroom.

Your maidenly sister gave vent to an enormous sigh and said: "Well, I'm glad to know our *main* problem is solved!"

I hope you all appreciate the ladylike delicacy of your sister's instincts.

Father's own delicacy was manifested far less directly than his young daughter's. During Reid's sophomore year at Yale, in a "Memorandum to William F. Buckley, Jr." Father writes:

Jane tells me that Reid has quite extensive sideburns. When he started growing them I mentioned them to him very casually and he said that that was required of the Glee Club—which sounds rather extraordinary. If you could gently suggest to him that he remove them, it would be a great relief to the family. I would rather he would not belong to the Glee Club.

Father

Not long after this, however, Father, repenting his rebuke, sent out to the Phoenix Bank in Hartford, a

Memorandum for Mr. Fenniman:

It seems to be the consensus that Reid should be getting an allowance of $100.00 a month beginning in June, and that out of this he should be able to accumulate enough money to buy clothes and books and so on at the beginning of college; and that thereafter his room and board bills should be paid, and that in addition he should get $100.00 a month.

One or two of the children were so presumptuous as to suggest that Reid be given a lecture on the value of money and on the difficulty of acquiring it, which I will not pass on to Reid.

W. F. Buckley

For Father's atonements were as roundabout as his remonstrances.

Reid's small pomposities, when he was growing up, were a source of continuing joy and exasperation to Father, and at times his correspondence with or concerning Reid almost doubled the volume of mail at the Sharon Post Office. In 1939, for instance, when Reid was nine years old, Father wrote from New York:

My dear Reid:

I have just submitted your music to a music house here and have sold it for $1.00. I will give you the dollar when I get out to Sharon.

They fully agreed with you and with me that your music was a masterpiece.

Affectionately,
Father

When Reid was 15, he received a routine letter from a firm of certified public accountants, asking him to confirm his balance at the bank. Reid answered:

Dear Sirs:

In reply to your inquiries concerning my account at the Sharon National Bank, I have at the present date the above mentioned ———. I drew a check for the amount of ——— in late January: It was made out to Miss Celia Reilly. The recent bank statement sent to me by your firm confused the issue as you see by crediting my account for ———. I delayed answer till the matter was cleared up. I received word from C.R. that she had as yet not cashed my check a few days hence.

I would appreciate it if you informed me what your business is with me: purely a question of curiosity concerning why any person deems it necessary to become acquainted with my personal account.

Yours truly,
F. Reid Buckley

Impressed with the manly dignity of his reply, Reid sent a copy to Father, adding that "I do not intend in the future to tell anything about my pecuniary affairs to any company that feels it would like a bird's eye view of me financially." The episode filled Father with such fearful joy that he circulated one hundred copies of the correspondence to his relatives and friends.

Sometimes Father got into what can only be described as a rut, on a given subject. One of the longest was the "car" rut—probably because cars and Father always disliked each other intensely—and the car rut consisted of at least 12 memoranda dealing with their effect on character, on physique, on intelligence; their stupidity, brutality, malice and willful disobedience, etc. Only a few of these can be found, but the series seems to have started with the following letter to "My dear Jane":

We were having a general conversation last night and Priscilla said that you had recently found out that you were charged with your car. I suppose I didn't take the precaution to tell Mr. Fenniman that this was a graduation present from your mother and me. Would you drop me a note about this and confirm this sad news and tell me just what the price of the car was? I will send a check within the next week or two to the bank to reimburse your account. After this, when you get hard-up, you should always write me about it; I may not be able to help you but I can give you a lot of sympathy.

Lots of love,
Affectionately,
Father

Perhaps it was the memory of Jane's firm rejection of (a) a hunter (a horse that hunts), (b) a pearl necklace, (c) an ermine jacket in lieu of the car Father promised her in a moment of aberration, that reopened the smouldering feud. At any rate, the memos of the following two years were devoted almost exclusively to cars.

For instance:

I think there is entirely too much driving of cars by our children. It is not unusual for two or three cars to come into New York in a day. In the first place, the best and most sensible way of getting to New York is by train; that is how over 90 per cent of the people from Sharon move from one place to the other. The cars are extremely expensive, and they are dangerous as well. I am sure that there is a very large mileage registered on the car of every member of the family.

Outside of John and Priscilla, none of you has earned enough money to buy a car and I think that you should be very careful in your use of one.

Some of you have gotten into the practice of arriving swankily in a car and turning it over to Mr. Cronin [the Superintendent at Father's office in New York] to park, asking him to put up the dollar for parking charges. Anyone who hasn't a spare dollar, or having one fails to carry it in his pocket, should not be driving a car into New York.

I have thought of this matter a number of times, and I am sure your Mother has.

W. F. Buckley

Another memo, from Camden, South Carolina, this time:

Now that most of you have your own cars, and the so-called (by the children) "family cars" which suffered greatly during the War for many and varied reasons have been replaced with new ones, I hope you will all try not to age them too much during the coming holidays.

First of all, if those of you who are nicotine addicts should be overcome by your craving while you are driving, please use the ashtrays. While I agree with Mayor McCorkle that everything possible should be done to keep Camden clean, I also would like to keep the inside of the cars clean, so please do not throw papers and trash on the floor. Regarding the City of Camden, I feel that you are all old enough to make your own decisions.

Second, Ben Heath tells me the station-wagon should never be left out overnight. So if you use it in the evening, be sure it is put in the garage, no matter how exhausted you may think you feel when you come home. Moreover, be careful when you do put it away, because station-wagons have become too wide to enter normal garages.

Third, if you are unfortunate enough to scratch or dent a fender, report it to the main office. We carry expensive insurance policies to cover all damage over $50.00; any damage under that figure will be paid for by the responsible party.

I hope that none of you younger children will take the preceding sentence as a suggestion that you have only major accidents.

Affectionately,
Father

The following communication, circulated the summer after the war, was a mere recapitulation of several others.

Memorandum to the Buckley Children:

I have been much concerned of late with the apparent inability of any of you, at any time, to go anywhere on foot, although I am sure your Mother would have informed me if any of you had been born without the walking capacity of a normal human being.

A few of the older children, notably Priscilla, occasionally walk a few hundred yards behind a golf ball, but all the others "exercise" exclusively by sitting on a horse or in a sailboat.

Concurrently, I have noticed that the roads around Sharon are crowded with Buckley cars at all hours of the day and night, and it has been years since any of you has been able to get as far as the Town Clock, much less the Post Office without a car, or if under 16, a car and a chauffeur.

All the cars are left out every night in all kinds of weather, undoubt-edly because of the dangerous fatigue involved in walking from the garage to the house.

I think that each of you should consider a course of therapy de-signed to prevent atrophy of the leg muscles if only for aesthetic reasons, or you might even go to the extreme of attempting to regain the art of walking, by easy stages of course. The cars might then be reserved for errands covering distances of over fifty yards or so.

Affectionately,
Father

And a resigned protest to Bill's future father-in-law:

Memorandum to Austin C. Taylor:

I have tried for many years to interest my children in conventional sports, but I have not been very successful. Billy is easily the worst in this regard, having no interest in tennis, golf, or other activities which satisfy the great majority of the nation. If you expect to entertain him, you will find it necessary to furnish him with (1) a horse, (2) a yacht, or (3) a private airplane.

Aloïse joins me in affectionate regards to you and Babe.

Will

The Buckley children were at all times kept *au courant* with the life and times of their brother Bill, sometimes unkindly referred to as "The Young Mahster," by means of memoranda of which the following, dated May 25, 1941, is typical.

Memorandum to Aloïse et al.

You will all, no doubt, be glad to know that Billy has again achieved his high B average, and is subsequently back on the Millbrook School Honor Roll. The reason for this academic improvement is the fact that he has terminated all connections with *The Silo* and *The Mill* (and vice versa), has completely ostracized the piano, and has let Pantepec [Father's oil company] and the foreign situation go to the dogs.

It may come as a surprise, therefore, to some of them, that one of Father's "ruts" was critical of Bill, and lasted from the time Bill learned to write, at the age of six, till he learned to type, at the age of sixteen.

February 16, 1940

My dear Billy:

I think more strongly than ever that you should take hold of your handwriting situation and work on the new system along the lines that I had discussed with Miss Reilly. You will never be able to take your present handwriting and do anything with it, in my opinion. It is not very intelligent to go through life with a handwriting that people cannot understand. Aloïse has done that and has almost incapacitated herself for writing. I am sure that you will get down to work with Miss Reilly and correct this situation.

Affectionately,
Father

Again:

October 10, 1940

Mr. Edward Pulling
Millbrook School
Millbrook, New York

Dear Mr. Pulling:
My wife sent me a letter from Billy today which reminds me of his very illegible handwriting. He uses the backhand, very awkwardly, and it seems to me it will cause him a lot of inconvenience and annoyance in the future as well as retarding his speed in writing. I realize that such things as handwriting should have been taken care of long before a boy gets to Millbrook, but nevertheless I wonder if there is anything you could have done for Billy in this connection.

(Bill's handwriting is still illegible, but he types very well indeed.)
Any other criticism Father made of Bill positively reeks of insincerity. When the Young Mahster was 15, for instance, Father wrote:

My dear Billy:
In thinking over my letter to you it may have appeared very critical and I hope you did not take it that way. Your Mother and I like very much your attitude of having strong convictions and of not being too bashful to express them. What I meant was that you would have to learn to be more moderate in the expression of your views and try to express them in a way that would give as little offense as possible to your friends.

But the old filing cabinets are also crammed with testimony to the fact that Father's children were far more to him than a source of mingled amusement, exasperation, pleasure and disapproval. He loved them with a watchful and an anxious protectiveness which, moreover, was not in the slightest *laissez-faire*. Not that his children didn't make their own mistakes, but only after the long exchange of formal memoranda (in the Buckley family, the equivalent of a tooth-and-nail battle)

which invariably ended one memo short of the ungentlemanly
ultimatum which might have led to the discourteous refusal.

If Father noted in later years that Maureen still gobbled her
words, that Bill's handwriting was totally unreadable, and
Aloïse seemed never to emerge from a cocoon of cigarette
smoke; that, in fact, the barrage of memoranda he had shot at
his children had remained to a large extent unheeded, this was
no reason to desist. And so, from his hotel in Bad Gastein two
weeks before his death came an admonitory note to a 36-year-old
daughter.

My dear Priscilla,

Since you and Carol plan to spend several weeks in Mexico, I
think you should know that young ladies of good families do not go
unescorted in Mexico City. This is a custom I think you girls should
respect . . .

Affectionately,
Father

CHAPTER 4

Growing Up with the Buckleys

In December of 1947, under the prodding of their father, the Buckley children brought out the first issue of a family newspaper, The Grelmschatka (a contraction of the names of their two homes—Great Elm, in Sharon, Connecticut, and Kamschatka, in Camden, South Carolina), which Father expected would appear twice a year. It was published six times between 1947 and 1958, with Priscilla editing the first four and the final issue and Aloïse and Patricia editing Number 5. These were the years when most of the Buckleys graduated from college, got married, got jobs, and started raising families of their own. Their doings are chronicled by Aloïse Heath in a column called "The Buckleyana." For easier identification: Aloïse Heath was the eldest child, twenty years older than Carol, the youngest. The first eight children—Aloïse (Allie), John, Priscilla (Pitts), Jim, Jane, Bill, Patricia (Trish), and Reid—were each approximately 18 months apart in age. Maureen was three years younger than Reid, and Carol six years younger than Maureen. The Barn referred to in many of these articles is a barn adjoining the family home in Sharon, which Father bought shortly after the war (Second World) and remodeled for the convenience of married children and grandchildren, of whom there are now fifty.

To business. The Heaths, never noted, at least on the maternal side, for speed of accomplishment, established some sort of record last summer by taking five months to move from St. Petersburg, Florida, to West Hartford, Connecticut. Those five months were passed in Sharon, where we would probably still be if the family had not inconsiderately, not to say unceremoni- ously, moved to Camden, South Carolina. Let no one think that we were simply *boarding* there, however. In the absence of Mother and Father, who spent the entire summer lurking behind crags in Canada under the pretext of (a) waiting with Jane in Calgary before her babies were born, (b) being with Jane while her babies were born, and (c) staying with Jane after her babies (two) were born, I managed to fill Mother's place in Sharon—more than adequately, as everyone was too bashful to say—and, in fact, to improve on Mother by instilling in my sisters and sisters-in-law those principles of *laissez-faire*- ism, *chacun-à-son-gout*-ism, and *sauve-qui-peut*-ism for which my housekeeping is so justly famous. Also to my credit are two other accomplishments which I think of as unrivaled.

1. The installation, in the downstairs telephone closet, of a bulletin board, complete with attached (I thought) pencils, attached (I thought) pads, and attached (I thought) thumbtacks. This, as it turned out, contributed a great deal to the general good since it relieved most of us of the necessity of buying our own pencils and pads to lose. As for the thumbtacks, I know for a fact that at least three are now stored in the down- stairs telephone closet, in a corner, on the floor, and behind the card table that leans on the shelf. *You* know, the shelf we write messages on with the lipstick someone left summer before last.

2. My second project was the installation of twelve (12) mailboxes clearly labeled in indelible ink with the full names, correctly spelled (in the English language), of each individual and/or couple in the family. This, of course, handily provided each individual, and/or couple, with 11 *other* boxes in which to sort bills, circulars, appeals for funds, requests from the

Phoenix Bank for signatures by return mail, and other items of no immediate or, as a matter of fact, eventual interest. Inevitably, the person whose box happened to have been chosen for another's castoffs, removed them, along with his own cast-offs, to still a third box, and so forth so that by the sixth or seventh move, a certain amount of personal mail had been gathered in *en route*. This system brought us back within ten days to the comfy old-fashioned method of looking through *everybody's* mail to find your own, which is much more inter-esting anyway. The *things* you find out from a penny postcard.

1953:

Two years and ten children ago, the last issue of *Grelm-schatka* hit what we like to call "the newsstands." We admit the responsibility, apologize for the delay, admire Priscilla, and hope that all future memoranda from Father will be directed at other members of the family.

The elder members, Mother, Father, Allie, Ben, and Jim, who is elder by virtue of temperament, steeled themselves for Reid's and Betsey's wedding—the fifth in two years—with a five-week stay in Paris and environs. They returned to this country to find that the unmitigated pleasure of Betsey's acqui-sition was somewhat tempered by the news of (1) Jane's loss of her unborn baby and (2) John's admittance to and emergence from the Sharon hospital for painful and mysterious reasons—painful to John and mysterious to medical science. John's second painful experience of the summer was not only frustrating—he was called up as a reservist first lieutenant, during the prelude to the Korean war, as an expert French linguist. He then suf-fered the humiliation of being dropped from the call-up.

Sometime in the course of this same summer and fall—of 1951—Bill and Pat retired to Mexico, bought a beautiful house whose principal asset was a more than somewhat life-sized bust of Beethoven, and settled down intending to accumulate

several million dollars. Fortunately for the as yet unaccumu-
lated millions, the publication of Bill's book, *God and Man at
Yale*, forced his and Pat's reappearance in this country at in-
frequent intervals during the fall of 1951—a fall which was
also graced by Maureen's coming-out party, at which her
glamorous and charming elder sisters were amazed to find that
she was considered by the casual observer to be their superior
in charm and glamour—though lacking, of course, that mellow
quality which comes only with maturity.

Jim, this same fall, at last reached the point—long anticipated
by the rest of us—where his future dinner engagements ex-
tended beyond his two-year apartment lease. He therefore
bought a house in Guilford to act as a permanent address for
the convenience of his future hosts. Little did he know that
in a few short months he was to meet June, moon, croon, and
spoon all combined in the person of Ann Cooley for whom he
is sacrificing, in one fell swoop, his home, his business, and his
association with New Haven which has lasted off and on since
his freshman year at Yale, some hmmph years ago.

This wedding will be in the tradition of the more conservative members of the family who marry only roommates,
classmates, and close friends of their brothers and sisters, viz:—
Jane's marriage to Bill Smith, Jim's classmate at Yale Law
School; John's marriage to Ann Harding, who grew up with
Brent Bozell, who was Bill's best friend at Yale; Patricia's marriage to Brent Bozell, who was Bill's best friend at Yale and
who grew up with Ann Harding; Bill's marriage to Pat Taylor,
who was Patricia's roommate at Vassar. Jim, intrepid soul, is
marrying a girl who is the sister of his former Yale roommate
Dick Cooley, *and* the classmate of his sister-in-law Ann Harding, *and* the office-mate of his sister Priscilla. (Only those
dangerous radicals, Aloïse and Reid, have married individuals
unmarred by the family checkout.)

To regress (retrogress), Bill, on October 15, 1951—jealous,

doubtless, of Pitts's new job and Jim's new house—published his book *God and Man at Yale*, dedicated "to God, to Man, and to Yale, in that order." The country as a whole, even those who regarded the book as being well to the right of Bloody Mary and the Bourbons, was astounded at its brilliance and appalled at its vocabulary. We, as a group, were not; we were only surprised that 27,000 people in the country were bright enough to read it. Which brings us to the Sad Case of the Fallen Arches.

Our ever-charming Mother, whose high-arched feet are so aristocratic as to be positively royal, began, during the two-week period which immediately followed the publication of Bill's book, to suffer from alarming pains in the aforementioned feet. At the same time, the aforementioned arches began to develop a sag which can only be termed middle class. Finally, before all was lost, her story was dragged out of her. It seems that beginning on October 16—October 15 being Bill's publication date—Mother had assigned herself a daily beat covering Fifth Avenue from 25th to 92nd Street, and back down Madison to 25th Street. At each book store she passed, Mother entered, nonchalantly flipped through a best-seller or two, was visibly appalled at the trash people read nowadays, and asked the clerk if he had a really fine book she had heard of called something like *Man and God at Harvard*? was it? or Yale? In any case, the author's name sounded like William F. Butler, Jr. Or something. If the clerk answered no, which was the answer Mother expected, she was able to launch into her carefully rehearsed lecture—during the course of which it became apparent that she knew somewhat more about the book than was apparent in her opening gambits. Unfortunately for Mother's regal arches, the clerk usually answered yes, which gave her the choice of lamely answering: "How nice!" and exiting with dignity—or buying yet another copy of the book. Those of us who know Mother know that her conversation may be loony but is never lame, so, inevitably, she bought the book and resumed her trudge down the Avenue, sometimes accumulating 18 or 20 pounds of literature within a couple of blocks—hence the transfer from Gothic to Late Norman arches. How many of the 27,000 sales were accounted for by Mother personally is her secret. There are several locked closets in her room, though.

Bill, sometime in the course of this spring (1951), abandoned Mexico and its promised millions to accept a position as Associate Editor of the *American Mercury*, which he held until a slight difference of opinion about the Republican presidential nominee. His political preference for Robert Taft, shared by all of us, was actively promoted by Patricia and Brent, who, after a brief visit in San Francisco looking for law firms whose very existence would be imperiled without the acquisition to the staff, in 1953, of one Brent Bozell, attended the Republican National Convention in Chicago. (The result of this convention, incidentally, caused our emotional sisterinlaw Ann Harding Buckley to hurl an extremely large book at an extremely expensive television set.) Trish and Brent, during their absence, left 18monthold Christopher, of the enigmatic smile, and sixmonthold Kathy, of the indestructible will, in the charge of Father, Mother, Allie, Ann, and Reid, who among them managed to create as many psychological problems as are possible in babies of the ages of the young Bozells. Bill and Pat, during this period, rejoicing in the peace and calm of those who do not summer at the Barn, bought and remodeled a beautiful house in Stamford, Connecticut, and, on September 28, became the parents of one Christopher Taylor Buckley, a child who is not only handsome and charming, like his mother, but well brought up, like his mother.

June saw an exodus to the Barn in Sharon by Ann, Allie, and Trish, who, with families, spent a placid summer around the swimming pool except for an incident precipitated by

Father. Our revered father, having been the guest of honor at an extremely gala party to celebrate his 71st birthday on July 11, took the occasion, on July 12, to come down with a severe case of mumps. Since he is a most dutiful grandfather, and hugs and kisses all grandchildren within reach daily, the follow' ing week was made hideous by the outcries of the eight young ones whose little bottoms were firmly injected with anti-mumps shots. However, not a mump was seen thereafter; as we men' tioned, he is a most dutiful grandfather. Father recovered in the pleasurable surroundings of Spain, Portugal, and France. He allowed Mother, Maureen, and Carol to accompany him, on the assumption that his physical well-being was more impor' tant than his nervous system. During his and Mother's absence, the big, beautiful reconverted Barn became big and converted.

Fall of 1952 saw a tragedy befall the family. We lost our baby. Carol entered the Sacred Heart Convent at Noroton, learned to put up her hair on bobby pins, learned to say "Ye Ga-a-ahds," and grew up. She has now attained the award of something called the "Green Ribbon" for qualities which are hazy to the layman, mysterious to her family, but extraordinar' ily impressive to Noroton students and alumnae. She is also the youngest student ever to have been accorded this honor, which is no more than the rest of us expected, well as we have trained her.

1958:

The four years since *Grelmschatka* last appeared have seen considerable progress made toward the fulfillment of Father's order, issued some time ago, that the Eastern Seaboard of the United States must and shall be chiefly populated by his descen' dants on or before January 1, 2050. Since June 1953, three three-year-olds, four two-year-olds, three one-year-olds, and two really *young* children have been obediently added to the family and one more (infant) is on order for the early part of

1958. All, naturally, are being brought up to think Cro-Magnon, vote Neanderthal, reproduce like mad, and read *National Review*.

Bill, of whose activities we have firsthand knowledge, spent half the summer of 1953 in Stamford, moodily writing his share of *McCarthy and His Enemies*, and the other half in Sharon, quarrelsomely rewriting Brent Bozell's. Brent vice-versa'd both geographically and emotionally. (None of us will ever forget the 14-hour-long argument, with the entire family ranged on one side or the other, as to which is the warp, which the woof of something. Nor can anyone remember what it was the warp or the woof *of*.)

Father, Mother, Maureen, and Carol were also in Europe that summer, the latter three in their accustomed role of escorts to the family's perennial Hay Fever Refugee—one might even say, King of Hay Fever Refugees. Mother was also in need of recuperation this particular summer, however. She had taken over the management of Aloïse's household for the month of June while Allie and Ben were in Europe, and had handled innumerable daily crises with her usual unruffled competence. Finally, though, a situation arose which had even Mother all shook up.

At three o'clock of a dark June morning, during a violent thunderstorm, Mother was confronted at the Big House by Allie's stout and pleasant cook, Jean, who had suddenly turned into two hundred pounds of gibbering lunacy. With hardly a quiver, Mother agreed fervently that it was indeed *very* wicked of everybody to be trying to kill Jean all the time and *very* wicked of her young husband to fall in love with 61-year-old Mademoiselle and *very* wicked of Mademoiselle to keep on squashing bugs and poisoning Jean with the bug juice; assured Jean that she would give all her enemies a good scolding in the morning; talked Jean into swallowing an inordinately large number of sleeping pills, and sent her back to bed. Only then did Mother alert the doctor and succumb to an uncontrollable fit of the giggles, which is as near hysteria as Mother ever gets.

Meanwhile, the "new Ann," as the grandchildren called (and call) Jim's unblushing bride, spent the summer alternating between Great Elm and the Gracie Square apartment which John's Ann (the "old Ann") had abandoned for the summer in favor of their Lakeville "campsite"—then being rebuilt for the second (third? fourth?) time. During the course of the summer Jim's Ann promptly lost her bridal status by becoming the future mother of Peter. She also established an ugly precedent of keeping such information to herself and thereby deprived herself of the benefit of the inexhaustible number of Helpful Hints which the mothers of the 16 children who preceded Peter in the family would have been only too happy to give her.

Aloïse spent 1954 in the study of mass abnormal psychology. As secretary of the "Committee for Discrimination in Giving," which had been formed by a small group of Smith graduates who believed in giving discriminately, she wrote a letter to the Smith alumnae asking whether they knew of the past and present pro-Communist activities of five members of the faculty; whether they approved or disapproved; and suggesting that those who disapproved ask the college authorities for an explanation before they dutifully forwarded the contributions which helped pay these professors' salaries. The suggestion that 27,000 American university women donate money according to the dictates of their consciences was considered not only highly inflammatory, but deeply subversive by the ladies, and the floodgates of public, private, and journalistic abuse were opened on Allie's surprised and unsophisticated head. (Needless to say, contributions to Smith College topped their previous all-time high by many hundreds of thousands of dollars.)

Maureen, however, in her senior year at Smith College, where all the witches were being hunted, found the ideological martyrdom visited upon her by her elder sister emotionally exhilarating but physically trying. For, as undergraduate representative of the Disloyal Alumna, Maureen had chosen "righteous serenity" as the attitude with which to face two thousand shocked undergraduates and three hundred disapproving professors—and, as we all know, the facial muscles used in expressing righteous serenity are unusually difficult to keep in position. However, the faculty, unwillingly cowed by her face and unwillingly impressed by her mind, unwillingly voted her a member of Phi Beta Kappa in the very midst of her family's disgrace—incredible as it seemed to Maureen's four elder brothers and four elder sisters, who are, as all of them know, *immensely* superior in intelligence.

Hartford housewifery and Smith studentery began to understand the mental aberrations of their otherwise harmless associates when it became known that Maureen's and Aloïse's BROTHER and BROTHER-IN-LAW had published a book called *McCarthy and His Enemies*, which was not only PRO-MCCARTHY, but ANTI his ENEMIES!! Bill and Brent launched their book at what can only be called a rollicking affair at the Waldorf, attended by Joe McCarthy, J. B. Matthews, Raymond Moley, John Chamberlain, Frank Chodorov, George Sokolsky, Westbrook Pegler, Howard Rushmore, Roy Cohn, and other lights and shadows of the conservative world.

Friends, acquaintances, employees, and creditors of the Buckleys remember the rest of that winter as one during which radio aerials and television antennae were continually filled by voices, be they never so slurred, which turned out to be Bill, and images, be they never so blurred, which turned out to be Brent, or vice versa, or both—but which, in any case, had to be watched and listened to in their *entirety* by those who wished to continue to be the friends, acquaintances, employees, and creditors of the Buckleys. In any event, the boys veni-ed, vidi-ed, and, *we* think, vici-ed, most of the well-known intellectual-type liberals of this country, and by the end of the winter, the "I-Can't-Stand-Bill-Buckley Club" had been expanded from Yale-lovers to include McCarthy-haters. You can imagine how exclusive that made *our* club.

The country woman who said: "I never feel like it's spring till the house is cleaned, the garden planted, and the baby born," was probably a Buckley woman, or, at the very least, married to a Buckley man. (A Buckley woman would have said "as if.") Jim's Ann produced Peter Pierce Buckley in April 1954 (after our prudent James, too considerate to inconvenience their obstetrician, phoned Aloïse in Hartford at 3:30 A.M. to describe certain unmistakable symptoms manifested by his wife and inquire as to the advisability of taking her to the hospital).

Mary Alison Heath was born in May to the Secretary of the "Committee for Discrimination in Giving" and has proved such a satisfactory child that she is known in the Heath family as the product of the "Committee for Discrimination in Having."

Priscilla, at United Press in Paris, an ocean away from the "high blood" producing elections in this country, was able to concentrate less on the cutting political diatribe and more on the soft answer which turneth away wrath—as, for instance, the case of the Parisian truck driver who ran through a stop sign and into the side of Pitts's car. Our temperate sister, having ascertained that her machine was undamaged, gave the truck driver a reassuring wave of the hand and drove on. This attitude, which is absolutely unprecedented in the history of the French horseless carriage, resulted in Priscilla's being chased for three blocks, caught at a stop light, and hairily kissed through the car window by the grateful teamster. Thus does the Old World repay its courtesies—in degree, if not in kind.

John and Ann spent their usual uneventful summer in Lakeville, hiring and firing maids, buying and selling cars, acquiring and disposing of dogs, and polluting Lakeville Lake through the medium of their highly eccentric septic tank. It is further rumored that the editor of the *Lakeville Journal* (who lies awake till four o'clock every morning reviewing John's latest "Letter to the Editor" and planning various lingering deaths for him) spent several chilly nights paddling up and down John's shoreline, trying to collect enough dead fish to have him arrested as a health menace. Ann, meanwhile, when aesthetics permitted, gave a series of large, quarrelsome cocktail parties, at all of which she aggressively maintained that the Buckleys had *many* lovable traits, even Bill, and that Bill's forthcoming magazine was not going to be nearly as bad as the identity of its publisher would lead one to believe.

The publisher-to-be of *National Review*, this summer, his normally acid personality heavily candied with charm, was winding up many weary months of raising the wherewithal for a publication to publish. Bill talked, listened, interviewed, and was interviewed all over the country, finding, not to his surprise, that 99.003 per cent of those who had indicated that they were strongly in support of a conservative weekly turned out to be not quite $o $trongly in $upport as they $hould have been. Bill's ruthless exploitation of his ever-obliging wife, on the grounds that Pat was prettier, is a tale far too sordid to be told here. Let us say only that Patricia, after trying 157 different shades of hair, settled on a dashing silver gray as the most suitable for a publisher's wife, and she has, for almost three years now, been true to her color—in *spite* of the distinguished gentleman who congratulated her on "growing old gracefully."

Had Carol been under the tutelage of any but the Sacred Heart nuns, who, it is rumored, pray nightly for the canoniza-tion of anyone related to St. William F. Buckley Jr., her school career might have been seriously endangered when it became known that that irresponsible brother-in-law of hers, Leo Brent Bozell, had left his safe, sound, secure, and staid job in a San Francisco law firm to become assistant counsel for Senator

McCarthy during the famous Senate trial by the Watkins Committee. McCarthy's denunciation of the Committee as "the
unwitting handmaiden of Communism" was part of a speech
written for him by our very own little Brent and, according
to leading political analysts, it was this very phrase which
absolutely but completely cinched McCarthy's censure. Joe,
overcome by the verbal gift of a man who could accomplish
with five words what hundreds of thousands of articles and
editorials could only attempt, immediately hired Brent as his
speechwriter and general assistant.

John and Ann's European jaunt inevitably brought them to
Paris, where they arrived barely in time to pull Priscilla out
of an incipient nervous collapse. Pitts, in the course of her
duties at the United Press, had become the office religious
expert because of her quaint custom of eating fish on Friday,
in spite of the fact that she was an intellectual-type Catholic.
And since Billy Graham is "religious" and Priscilla is "religious," she was considered by her superiors eminently suited
to cover Billy's "conversion" of Paris, and to deliver, every 24
hours, the three glowing Billy Graham stories demanded by
the U.P.'s Southern Baptist newspaper subscribers. Unfortunately, Priscilla's conscientious coverage and dutiful reportage
led to what can only be described as "giving scandal"—a venial
sin, to be sure. It happened that on the final night of Billy
Graham's big push, Pitts, on her way up the aisle to confer
with the great man's press agent, found herself inextricably
melded, to her horror, in the queue of those who had "made
the decision for Christ." The cordial welcome of her fellow-
queuists, plus the good-mannered cowardice (sometimes called
the cowardly good manners) innate in the Buckleys, plus the
further fact that withdrawal from the line of those who had
"made the decision" could only mean that one had *not* made
the decision, kept Pitts in the company of the saved until the
ever-narrowing gap between herself and a tenderly beaming

Billy Graham deacon panicked her into undignified flight followed by the understanding glances of those who know a real sinner when they see one.

Reid, on the other hand, joined the ranks of the saints that winter—even if only the ranks of the post-Reformation, Adam Smith-canonized saints. Forsaking wife, sons, and Sharon, at least for five days a week, he took a job as assistant editor of *The Freeman*, in which he wrote what in some issues seemed to be all the book reviews and half the articles to boot. Reid's Period of Conformity lasted from December to June, when an *intime*, not to say psychiatric, session with his checkbook disclosed the information that his salary minus the cost of his bachelor quarters in Irvington minus the cost of the handyman-yardman who expensively pinch-hit for the Young Master in Sharon, showed him to be working for approximately 19 cents an hour. Reid—ever a sharp man with figures—then came to the conclusion that the comforts of home and family were worth at *least* two bits an hour, and returned forthwith to wife, sons, Sharon, and the unpublishable novel.

Father chose Betsey Heath's birth-date to behave in an extremely trying manner—even for Father.

"Favver," as most of his grandchildren call him, was operated on in April 1955; went into shock shortly thereafter, and topped off the whole episode with a rather severe stroke, which partially paralyzed him. In short, within ten days or so, he went through enough crises to kill off several ordinary men. The doctors, under the illusion that they were dealing with just one ordinary man, summoned the family, which arrived *en masse* (except for Aloïse, who was needed at home to give birth to Betsey) and occupied most of a Charlotte, North Carolina, hotel floor for two weeks, alternately twiddling their thumbs and holding Mother's hand. The doctors, after a while, began to be a little shaken in their diagnosis by the increasing sassiness of Father's remarks to the prettier of the nurses, during his lapses into consciousness, and they were finally forced to admit point-blank that Father had made liars out of them. (There are few more pitiful sights than a doctor apologizing for the fact that his patient didn't die.) However, the medical profession continued to believe that anything that would kill an ox would kill Father, and for well over a year issued crisis calls at regular intervals. Finally, Father himself, realizing that the only way to get rid of the hordes of relatives who kept gathering gloomily at his bedside was to stop giving them the incentive to gather, made up his mind to get well, and forthwith did so. Mother, who had gone through this entire period with the extraordinary courage and stamina of which only she is capable, gave several sighs of relief, a great many prayers of thanks (it is rumored that Mother's rosary quota is now up to 71 a day) and settled back into her old role of chief target of Father's witticisms. We all knew Father was recovering when he began to make sarcastic remarks to Mother; we knew he *had* recovered when Mother began to make sarcastic remarks back.

In the meantime, life, oddly enough, kept rolling along. Maureen went to Bad Gastein, in Austria, with Father, Mother, and entourage in August (a non-crisis month) of 1955, at which time, Maureen tells us, "I was given my very first opportunity to take the water cure." Maureen was also assigned the task of entertaining the "young son" of her parents' nightly canasta partners: an endearing boy who, besides being an Arab prince, was 42 years old and mentally retarded. Maureen further reports that one evening the Arab prince suddenly turned into the Sheik of Araby, and she was given her very first opportunity to establish that, given sufficient incentive, any girl can outrun any man straight up the side of a Tyrolean Alp.

The summer over, Mother and Father returned from Europe with Maureen—who had botched her very first opportunity to become a Maharanee—and the family spent the early part of the fall holding its breath till the publication of *National Review*'s first issue. (Except Bill, that is; Bill was trying to catch his breath.) The really, truly physical appearance of *National Review* meant that the Christophers, who were still allowing Father Keller to run things, lost Maureen, as they richly deserved to do, and United Press, which continued to honor talented females with impressive titles instead of legal tender, lost Priscilla, as *they* richly deserved to do. On November 19, 1955, a *National Review* heavily loaded (but *certainly* not *over-loaded*, according to our ever-loving mother, whose favorite sentence is: "I simply have to *face* the *facts: All* my children are talented!") with Buckleys brought out its maiden issue. The new weekly was, to nobody's surprise, acclaimed by the national press with a silence of deafening proportions. Six months, or about 28 issues, later, *National Review* had become so well known, and was publicly referred to so often by people who didn't know they weren't supposed to, that the national press was forced to nod stiffly in the direction of its junior member. Several magazines, accordingly, published detailed analyses of *NR*, mentioned the joyful anticipation (*secret* anticipation, obviously) with which they had awaited the addition of a conservative periodical to the national scene, and dwelled on the genuine regret they felt when they realized that *National Review* was not the answer to their prayers. For, they all explained, *National Review* was not *really* conservative; real conservatism was more liberal.

CHAPTER 5

The Day Maureen Was Born

Maureen's *arrival in the family was eagerly awaited by her older brothers and sisters who found their mother extraordinarily tardy in this matter. The first eight Buckley children had been born at 18-month intervals; they had to wait three full years for Maureen's advent. Her successor, Carol, would be quiet and biddable. But Maureen was pugnacious and invited teasing. She responded with indignation, and when driven too far would plant her feet apart, arms akimbo, blonde pigtails flying, cheeks red with rage, and denounce her tormentor. "You can go up de Hill," she would say, her grasp of English being insecure. She was brought up speaking Spanish. This was her version of "go to Hell." This story is about the day she was born.*

I was 14 the April day Maureen was born. The other members of the Big Four, John, Priscilla, and Jimmy, were 12, 11, and ten. We were all unapproachably, superciliously, who-is-this-worm-I-see-before-me-ly, veterans of English boarding schools. Jane, at nine, was a lonely little Lady Fauntleroy daily displayed on long, slow walks through the town. Bill was seven, and had for some months been awaiting a reply to his formal request that the King of England pay his war debts to the United States. Patricia and Reid, who were to be Maureen's "best friends" within the family, were six and four and masters of the red-headed art of sudden sunny wrangles with which they enlivened the soft monotony of nursery days.

But I was the best. I was 14, and in honor, perhaps of my age, perhaps of my coming status as the eldest of nine children, not merely eight, I was to spend the day in Paris with Mother, who was waiting for the baby in a hotel. (Father was in New York, Making Money.) As an introduction to the world of responsible womanhood, Mademoiselle put me on a second-class carriage in the little railway station at Chantilly, where Maureen's siblings were spending their Easter holidays, seated me next to a billowing farm woman whose creaking black lap supported the basket-nest of a mother hen and her irrepressible yellow babies, and after warning me at some length and in unnecessarily loud whispers to place no confidence in nuns, whose guise was frequently assumed by white-slavers, left me quite, quite alone for the forty-minute journey. There, at the other end of the line, in showery, sparkling, springtime Paris, was Mother, aglow with welcome and simultaneously— Mother can do these things—glaring suspiciously at every man (but not, in her innocence, at every nun) who shared the Gare-St. Lazare with her irresistible daughter, ravishingly clad in The Middle School uniform of St. Mary's Convent, So. Ascot, Berks. Mother had, as usual, a Plan: "... the most *wonderful* idea, darling, We'll have the baby *today*—it's Patricia's sixth birthday, you know," and as a special holiday treat, I would stay in Mother's hotel overnight and be the *first* to see the baby. In fact, I would be the baby's godmother, O joy, O rapture, O acme of grown-uptitude! Still, in order to practice the weary cynicism I rehearsed nightly before the mirror: "Exactly *how* was this to be arranged?" I drawled Britishly. "Nothing to it, darling. I'll manage," said Mother airily: and Mother managed, as Mother manages.

Not the rocky, rocky road of Tristan to Isolde or Ghent to Aix was rockier than the road from Mother's arrangements to Maureen's acquiescence, however. One reason, of course, was that she ordered the taxi driver to take us for a two-hour drive over the most *rocher*-filled streets in Paris, and, although *rochers* may mean *rocks* to a lady whose native language is English, they mean *boulders* to a gentleman whose native language is French. But boulders moved not Maureen, nor discouraged Mother, who, immediately after our return to the hotel, ordered "deux valises pleines de livres" from Room Service, and carried them up and down the room until I was seasick. ("Just for a mile, dear . . . the same number of steps as between the Etoile and the Louvre," Mother assured me breathlessly.)

To the last, Maureen retained her integrity and, refusing to allow herself to be immolated on the altar of Patricia's sixth birthday, allowed herself to be given birth to at three o'clock on the morning of April 24th, when she made her appearance wearing skin of a seasoned yellow, bright as the daffodils in the flowercarts under her window. Her first words were equally jaundiced. At the age of one hour, when she was put into my arms, she stared at me insolently, and said, "Nyanh, nyanh."

Barely two years later, she completed the sentence, which was to be her favorite for almost a third of her life. "*Nyanh, nyanh,*" she said. "*You fink you're so big.*"

The following passage was found in a notebook of Aloïse Buckley Heath after her death. It was a tentative introduction to the long piece she had intended to write for a book about her younger sister, Maureen Buckley O'Reilly, who died in 1964 of a cerebral hemorrhage, leaving her husband, Gerry O'Reilly, and five children, the oldest of whom was five. She was thirty-one.

How do you tell a little girl grown that you saw the tears she scrubbed so angrily from her eyes last summer, the day you teased her too much and too cruelly. How can you say you're sorry when that little girl is gone; for the day she cried was last summer, when she was barely ten, and this is a day in May, and she is already eleven. The shamed and shameful tears are lost in the small busyness of her small past, but not in yours. Never, now, in yours.

How do you ask a poised young woman to forgive the bright flush you brought to the cheek of an eager girl who proposed to share with you her discovery of one of life's older verities; and whose eyes you dulled with a little mocking word. Now she is a college woman, knowledgeable, discriminating, sophisticated; and only you remember the quaver that once underlay the young girl's bright confidence.

How do you tell your sister you love her, when your sister is dead.

CHAPTER 6

A Letter for Maureen

[A short story]

There isn't any doubt about it, Maureen *is* different.

People are always asking me why my poor little sister Maureen is already at boarding-school at the Tender Age of 13 when the Older Girls didn't go till they were 15, and it is hard to Go Into Details without having people think one is long-winded, so I usually just say it's because she's different. Which is true.

My Mother, who is a married lady of some fifty years and a Kindly Heart, says it is because Maureen is a seventh child, and then all the Big Ones—I am one of the Big Ones; I, Ritchie, am 14, one year older than Maureen—get sad, understanding looks on their faces and say things like: "Oh, so *that's* it!" and "I'm beginning to *see* now!" and "Well, that explains *every-thing!*" Then Maureen always gets mad and says: "Oh, you think you're all so smart," which is really just another way of showing how different she is, because when you say a thing like that it means you have no Sense of Humor, a very important thing to have in our family. (I have a Sense of Humor, but not Fully Developed.)

The most peculiar way Maureen shows her differentness is about Getting Things Done. Getting Things Done is the second most important thing in our family after a Sense of Humor. It is only the second most important thing because it is our Weak Point—except for Maureen—and nobody considers that his Weak Point is the most important. Naturally, Maureen thinks Getting Things Done comes first, since this is her Strong Point, and she was even, at one time, pretty puffed up about her ability along this line, but as Mother, who frequently puts things in a very acute, if old-fashioned, way, says: "Pride goeth before a fall." This, as it turned out, was All Too True.

Maureen says that Getting Things Done is like a lump in her mind that keeps on *being* there till she does whatever she's supposed to do. Anybody can see from this that Maureen has always been very good and a Great Favorite with Mother and Father. The Big Ones—I am one of the Big Ones—say she will grow out of this, but I don't know. She is already thirteen.

For instance, Maureen *always* answers letters. The rest of us sometimes get the answers to letters written out, but we practically never get them written *and* addressed *and* stamped *and* mailed.

Of course, the rest of us being the Way We Are about answering letters, Maureen had to be born the Other Way. *Her* Inner Compulsion is twice as compelling as John's and it lasts much longer—in fact till she gets an answer to her letter, which she says is the only sure proof that the person she wrote to, got it. And then it starts all over again. As John says, Maureen answers letters with the Speed of Light, and it is therefore considered very dangerous, in our family, to enter into a correspondence with her.

All that would be all right if Maureen would confine herself to answering her own letters, but to show you how she Carries Things to Extremes, she even answers other people's mail if she thinks they take too long. Last summer vacation, for instance, she answered Mr. Millbrook's letter to me and said, yes, I would try to do better at Math next year, which wasn't what I would have said at *all*. I was going to explain to him

about planning to be a Prominent Author and hence not need-
ing mathematics. And then, in spite of what I said to her—and
I can be Extremely Withering—just because she heard Mother
say something to Father about "You'd better do something
about your Income Tax" and Father said "What Income?",
Maureen took it upon herself to write the Collector of Internal
Revenue—who is an Unrelenting Enemy of our Family anyway—and say that Father had no Income and please stop
bothering him. As I pointed out to her afterwards, this certainly
could not have added to the respect in which our Father is
held by the United States Government.

But the worst thing Maureen did along that line was four
years ago when she was nine, which shows how young these
things develop. Our sister Sally, who is our First Child and
First Girl, got married and when she didn't get around to
writing a thank-you note for the last wedding present that
dribbled in, Maureen wrote it for her. The lady she wrote it
to sent Maureen's letter back to Mother with Caustic Comments, which is how we know. It said: "Dear Mrs. Lavatory"
(the lady's name is La Vetrie), "How could you be so gennerus
to a poor young bride like me? I opened your package with
fear and tremling. Could it be what I had longed for and yerned
for and hoped for and dreemed about? Could it be a pickle
fork? It was. It was. How sweet. I thank you. A big kiss from
Sally." Can you imagine? We were A Laughing-Stock! The
whole town laughed at us; even Mother and Father and the
Big Ones laughed. Of course I did, too, but only because I
have a good Sense of Humor.

This summer a terrible thing happened to Maureen, which
is what this story is really about. John says I should call it
"Caught in the Meshes of Her Own Efficiency," but I think
that's too long. Father said John could rest secure in the knowledge that nobody would ever write a story about *him* called
that, but then that was the day that John found the missing

key to the car had been in his pocket all along, and Father was naturally Bitter. Anyhow, the thing that happened was that Maureen wrote a letter to the Pen-Pal Department of some dopey kid-magazine she is always reading, and it got published. The letter said: "Dear Pals: My name is Maureen Stoddard and I am 13 years old, nearly. I have blue eyes and my hair is almost blonde. I am 4 Ft. and 11 In. and I weigh 96 Pds. I have a brown horse called Jim and a brown and white dog called Jimmy and a yellow cat called James. My favorite name is Jim. Ha Ha. My brother Ritchie [that's me] works in the zoo at his school and every summer he brings home a flying squirrel and a python and I take care of them. [Not entirely true.] I also have nine brothers and sisters, six older and three younger. A big kiss from Maureen Stoddard, Age 13."

Maureen, of course, being such a nit-wit, thought the Pen Pals column was just for people to read in the magazine. She didn't know that Pen Pals are people who write each other. As I often tell her, if she'd only ask the advice of older persons occasionally, which I'd be only too glad to give, she wouldn't get into these messes.

Anyhow, her letter was printed, principally, I imagine, because of my flying squirrel and python. Maureen showed us the letter in the magazine on the 22nd of June. I remember distinctly because it was Bob's 19th birthday—Bob is our Fourth Child and Second Boy—and Maureen was broke, so instead of a birthday present she gave him a promise to make all his appointments, like dentists and dates, all summer long, and to Remind him. John said that wasn't a promise, that was a threat, and Bob said a better birthday present would be to promise not to Remind him, and Mother and Father said it was a Fine Idea. So we had quite a discussion all during lunch, and it only ended when Maureen, who is very illogical, said maybe we all thought we were very smart, but she had the first Published Works of the family because she had a letter in Pen Pals. She showed it to us then, in a very red and flustered way, so we Remembered Our Manners, which we often do, and told her it was very good. John even said it was a very Telling piece of writing, and would probably Call Forth a Response. Little did we know.

That was on a Tuesday. On Thursday Maureen got seven letters from Pen Pals.

On Friday she got eighteen.

Between Saturday and the following Tuesday she got 47 more.

By the first of July, Maureen had had 115 answers to her letter, and they were still coming in. I guess if you haven't got the point of this by now you never will, but just in case you haven't, the point is this. Maureen *has* to answer letters. Her Inner Compulsion makes her.

So there she was, stuck. Enmeshed, as John and I would say.

The first day she worked all morning and took off in the afternoon to go swimming. The second day—she'd had 25 letters by then—she worked all morning and went upstairs again right after lunch and wrote till five. By the third day she had made the Appalling Discovery that she couldn't keep up with her correspondence unless, besides all that, she worked till nine o'clock at night, which is bedtime in our family for Growing Children.

For the next week we hardly saw Maureen at all. She got Ella, who is our maid, to give her her meals in her room, and whenever you looked in, there she was, on her stomach in the middle of the floor, writing and writing, with a small pile of answered letters by her left elbow and an enormous pile of unanswered letters by her right elbow. John called them the Mountain and the Molehill. She didn't go swimming once in a whole week. She didn't ride her pony. Her eyes got red, her hair got messy, and her face, which is usually pretty lobstery in the summer, got pale. She even almost got thin. In fact, she looked like a word that when you use it, it does not show that you are Bold and Daring but only that you have an Inadequate Vocabulary. And four times that week, at bedtime, when I absent-mindedly ran my thumb across her toothbrush—which I sometimes do for the Younger Ones, to Protect Them Against Themselves—her toothbrush was dry. And the third most important thing in our family, after a Sense of Humor and Getting Things Done, is Brush Your Teeth Twice a Day. So that shows what a state she was in.

And still the letters were coming in, piles and floods of them. The Older Girls took turns at night, massaging Maureen's writing hand with skunk oil, which though not aesthetic is efficacious. This means, does not smell good, but feels wonderful.

In the meantime, our family relations were going to pot. Mother and Father had an argument in front of us, which anybody ought to know is Bad Psychology and Breaks up the Harmony of the Home. Father said that the terrible thing which had happened to Maureen was Good Character Training, and Mother said, yes, but the Child's Health Comes First. Mother said all work and no play makes Jack a dull boy— Mother often says awfully good things; I take after Mother in many ways—so they finally decided that Maureen could work all day, but she had to come downstairs for meals and she couldn't work after supper. The Big Ones were always after Maureen to just give up and not answer any more letters, but Mother and Father naturally could not do this because of the way they feel about Getting Things Done. I didn't even try to persuade her, for after all, I've known Maureen since I was a little over one year old, and I have had a lot of experience with her Inner Compulsions.

It was then that John and Matt, Sally's husband, did the things that I shall never feel the same towards them about. Matt *may* have been just trying to help, but of John's motives

I have the deepest suspicions. Anyhow, one morning, after
Maureen's nine-to-five schedule had started, Matt, who has a
Sense of Humor but is Fundamentally Kind, took her aside
and said that if her Inner Compulsion was going to keep on
acting so silly about these Pen Pal letters, she might as well
Face Facts and realize that for the next two or three years,
even if over half the Pals dropped out, she still would have
almost three hundred left and hence would be carrying on a
terrific correspondence. (Which is rather a sad way to have to
spend your Early Adolescence, but sooner or later, as I often
tell Maureen, we must all Attain Maturity.) Therefore, said
Matt, the thing to do was to learn to write very fast, to keep
her working time Down to a Minimum, and the fastest way
to write is to use the typewriter. So the idea was for Maureen
to learn to type as quickly as she could, which though it means
more work at first means less work in the long run, and hence
pays off. You can easily see from this that Matt has a Logical
Mind, and indeed, he has often told me that since he married
into our family I have been a Great Comfort. Maureen has not
a Logical Mind, but she is Easily Swayed, so from then on, at
five o'clock every afternoon, Matt gave her a typing lesson and
after supper she practiced till bedtime. Mother and Father
could not say anything to this because typing is Improving
Yourself, which is the fourth most important thing in our family.
However, Maureen's life began to get pretty dreary again and
her Personal Appearance, not to mention Hygiene, was once
more neglected. But she did not begrudge the extra time because
the answers to her answers had already begun to come in and
it was Readily Apparent that no one could see Where It Would
All End.

It was John, though, who started Maureen off on her Career
of Crime. *His* idea, he said, was as far superior to Matt's as is
Eternity to an Hour. Number One, he said, Maureen couldn't
just plain stop answering letters like a normal person, because

she wasn't Made That Way. Number Two, even if she got so that she could type two hundred and forty words a minute, which is the World's Record held by Billy Rose, she would still be doomed to a Life of Deadly Monotony. *But*, said John, if Maureen could find a way to make people stop answering *her* letters her problem was solved and once again she would be a Free Woman. At first, John said, he had thought of writing just very dull letters that would make the recipients unin-terested in carrying on the correspondence, but when he thought of the Mammoth Response to the original letter, he had realized that it would be impossible to be dull enough. I immediately recognized this as a Subtle Insult, but Maureen did not because she has not the Lightning Mind which charac-terizes some people.

His second and better idea, continued John, was for Maureen to make her handwriting so illegible that none of her Pen Pals could read it, which everyone knows cuts down tremendously on one's interest in answering letters. Which if John Marsh, who is my roommate at school ever reads this, now he knows why our summer correspondence is so one-sided.

I might as well tell you right away that although Maureen adopted this suggestion, even to the extent of practicing illeg-ible handwriting by flashlight for two hours every night after she went to bed, it did not work. All of her Pen Pals seem to have great experience with reading bad handwritings, because not one of them dropped out, even though Maureen got so illegible that she has to take special tutoring in Penmanship at school this year. However, the Harm Was Done. She got the idea of making the Pen Pals *stop writing her*.

First it was by legal means, if dumb. You've got to say this for Maureen, in fact I later said it myself to Lieutenant Grant of the State Police, she tried every other way first, and Lieuten-ant Grant, with all his experience, should know how Desperate a Desperate Woman can become. The failure of her postcards showed her that only Extreme Measures would be Effective. The postcards were penny ones without pictures, which Maureen said would show Extreme Poverty, and she bought 520 of them, because that was how many correspondents she then had. On each of the postcards—except for two which went to the same town, which she made different, which was my idea—she wrote:

"Dear Pen Pal Joey:" (or Martha or Polly or Sam, depending on what their name was) "My Mother and Father are both very ill from Measles and Beri-beri, so I have to get a job to support our family who are in Dire Need, so I will not have time to write any more letters. I am sorry it all had to end like this. A big kiss from your use to be Pen Pal, Maureen Stoddard, Age 13."

This, of course, was Practicing Deceit, which older persons understand is only permissible if you laugh at the end of oral deceit or write "Ha Ha" at the end of written deceit. On my suggestion, therefore, Maureen wrote "Ha Ha" very, very small on the place where the stamp goes on top, so her conscience didn't feel quite so bad as it otherwise would have. As for the penny postcards to Indicate Extreme Poverty, that was not deceit, because by this time Maureen was extremely poor, paper, ink, and stamps having Made Inroads on her allowance to the extent of a cool $11.44, which she had borrowed from me. (I am the only one in our family who always has money, even towards the end of the month, and when the Big Ones make sarcastic remarks about Scrooge, who is a character in a book, I always reply quite calmly and coolly that some people Spend Money Foolishly and some do not.)

Maureen's postcards only proved, however, that Crime, even in a small way, Does Not Pay, and you'd think she would have learned something from this which Future Events proved she did not. From then on for the rest of the summer, packages started to come in along with the letters and every single package was full of something awful, though you could see that the people who had sent them's intentions were Of the Best. I catalogued the presents as they arrived, since I am By Nature Methodical, and this is what Maureen got:

```
 43  dozen prs. socks
  9  slips
  3  dresses
  2  sweaters
  1  corset with bones
  1  cake
  5  boxes of cookies—(2 very good)
102  nickels    ⎫
 47  dimes      ⎬  (adds up to No Mean Sum)
  1  dollar bill ⎭
  1  book called "The Girls' Book of Handicraft"
```

This last was the only thing that was in fairly good condition, which did Maureen no good because when Father found out—and he finally did in spite of a Conspiracy of Silence—he made Maureen send back everything that wasn't actually falling to pieces including the money she had spent and the food she had eaten. My Father is a Very Proud Man.

You can easily see that Maureen's postcards were an Utter Flop and did not Lighten Her Load in any way, because she now had packing and shipping to do besides her regular correspondence, and her regular correspondence was increased by large numbers of older sisters and Mothers who had read her postcards and took pity on her sad plight and wrote pages and pages of helpful advice. Who can Cast the First Stone then if Maureen was, as I have said before, Driven to Desperation?

One day, about two weeks after the postcard business, Ella, our maid, came upstairs to Father's room and said that Lieutenant Grant of the State Police was in the living-room waiting to see him. Now, visits from Lieutenant Grant and other members of the State Police are not entirely unknown in our family, due to the fact that some of the people in Sheraton, who have not our Highly Developed Sense of Humor, do not see the funny side of our jokes, and sometimes take unkind measures, so Father was not as astonished as some Fathers might have been.

Lieutenant Grant said he had a very distressing thing to tell Father. Which was that, the night before, the alarm from the Sheraton Post Office had rung in the State Police barracks in Canaan. All the policemen jumped in the police cars and with their sirens screeching raced 15 miles over to Sheraton in 22 minutes, Endangering Life and Limb, as Lieutenant Grant said. And when they broke into the Post Office, revolvers in their hands and terror in their hearts, who should they find but nobody! And it was only after searching for twenty minutes that they found Maureen, who, though fat, is little, crouching in the Out-of-Town bin. You can imagine their Complete Consternation! Also their Fury and Dismay.

State Policemen are as a rule, I have found, kindly Men, sometimes even Fathers and Grandfathers, but, of course, they would not be Policemen did they not have a sterner side to their natures. And it was the sterner side that Maureen, though often called an Appealing Child, drew forth. After they removed her from the Out-of-Town bin, in which she had become stuck due to excessive fatness, they took a very firm attitude toward her. They asked her how she got into the Post Office, and what she was doing in the Post Office, and what did she mean by the whole thing. All this they asked in No Uncertain Terms. Maureen answered that she had come in the window with no difficulty whatsoever; as to What She Was Doing, and What Did She Mean, she Remained Mute. Then Lieutenant Grant and his cohorts, after saying various intimidating things, went all through the Post Office and found that everything that should be locked was locked, which did not help.

After that they looked in the pockets of Maureen's dress and her school blazer and found nothing but a nickel, which they figured, Father being a Gentleman of Means, she did not have to break into the Post Office to get, and a Rose Pomade Lipstick, which I have long suspected. Maureen told me that at this time she said, "Unhand me, sir," very often and very loudly, because that is what the ladies say in Rafael Sabatini, which Maureen is a Constant Reader of. They finally did unhand her, due more, I think, to there being no more pockets to go through than to Maureen's Sharp Words. Then one of the other officers suggested that they take Maureen back to the Police headquarters, and have a matron search her all the way down to her Bare Skin, which Lieutenant Grant said "Better Not" to, the grandfatherly side of his nature having, I suppose, returned, causing him to remember that the Stoddard girls are Well Brought Up and hence modest. After that they asked Maureen over and over and over to tell them why she was in the Post Office, which Maureen said is the Third Degree; but anyone with Knowledge of the World knows that it is impossible to hold a Third Degree without the use of strong spotlights and rubber hoses, which the policemen must have absent-mindedly left behind them in Canaan. On the contrary, towards the end they gave her chewing gum and patted her on the head and pled, actually pled with her to tell them just a little something to write down in their notebooks. But after an hour or so of silence on the part of Maureen, it was plain to be seen that she had a Will of Iron, so when she explained that it was almost nine o'clock and that it was an Inflexible Rule in our family that Growing Children should be in bed by nine, they let her go with, I imagine, Mixed Emotions. Maureen told me that Lieutenant Grant said:

"Well, run along home then, girlie. I'd hate to have you break a rule!"

In which I would have detected a Note of Sarcasm myself,

but as I may have mentioned, Maureen was not born with those Powers of Keen Observation with which some people were.

After Lieutenant Grant finished his sad account, Father just sat for a little while. Then he sighed a long, shuddering sigh and he said in a Calm and Contained Voice:

"Ritchie, go and fetch Maureen."

His Calm and Contained Voice was only loud enough to reach behind the door where I happened to be at the time, for the First Duty of a Prominent Author is to Keep Well-Informed, but just on General Principles I answered: "Yes, Father," in a small and faraway voice as if I were just coming from the kitchen, and I went up to Maureen's room.

Maureen was Hard at Work at her new system for licking stamps, which is to dip her tongue in a glass of milk and then to quickly slide a stamp across it. She says this is Pleasant and Nutritious, and I say, maybe so, but it is not Pleasant to Look At.

I took her downstairs to the living-room, watching her face all the time for Significant Reactions, which there were none. But when I started to go into the living-room with her, in my Big-Brotherly way, Father said:

"I don't think this small matter is worth taking up your valuable time, thank you, Ritchie."

I interpreted this as a Strong Hint to leave the room which I did because I am quick to take a hint, especially from Father, but then he shut the door, so I am afraid that for this scene I must depend on Hearsay Evidence, which, after all, is Better Than Nothing.

My Hearsay Evidence—and to some small extent the Evidence of My Ears, which could not help overhearing Father's and Lieutenant Grant's voices after a while—is all to the effect that Maureen continued her policy of Remaining Mute. I could not help thinking that under Similar Circumstances I would

have Played the Scene quite differently—which is not un-
natural, for it is universally admitted that I have a Flair for
the Dramatic. Here was a situation which positively Cried For
Acute Laryngitis or Symptoms of Amnesia, and all Maureen
could think of was Open Defiance!

In any event, her policy of Remaining Mute came to Naught.
For just as Father opened the door again, looking as warm and
frustrated as I've ever seen him look, the phone rang. Father
answered it himself, though not a Usual Practice with him,
but he did it, I suppose, to get away from an Impossible Situation. The phone call threw Considerable Light on the matter.
It was from Mr. Moore at the Post Office. He said that in the
Out-going Bin, Somewhat the Worse for Wear, he had found
102 letters addressed to Maureen. On all the letters Maureen's
name and address were crossed out, and each of them was
stamped "Address Not Known" and "Return to Sender," with
the Post Office's Official Stamp. Whereas, said Mr. Moore, he
knew darn well where Maureen was and equally darn well
that he didn't stamp those letters himself.

It took but a moment for Father, with the Keen Perceptions
common to the males in our family, to realize that this was the
work of None Other than Maureen, which I personally thought
would have been quite a fine idea if Our Postmaster had not
been so efficient. Father explained it all to Mr. Moore, who
Agreed not to Prosecute, and then he explained it all to Lieutenant Grant, who said Girls Will be Girls and departed with No
Hard Feelings. So that was the end of that incident except
that for the next week or so Mother and Father went out of
their way to be nice to Maureen, which is how you tell, in
our family, that Mother and Father are Very Much Annoyed.
When they are especially nice, it means that they have said
such Hard Things about you to each other that they are feeling
the Pangs of Remorse. (And for the benefit of the Younger
Members of the family I will add a friendly hint to the effect

that the best time to touch them for a Raise in Allowance is immediately after you have done Something Awful.)

Maureen, however, in spite of the way Everything Turned Out All Right, will never feel the same toward either Lieutenant Grant or Mr. Moore, who, she says, are Confirmed Busybodies. An informal talk on my part as to their duties to the United States Government was to Little or No Avail.

My Mother has a very good way of putting things, and she often says: "It never rains but it pours." She means by this that if something happens, either bad or good, then something else, only more so, will happen too. So I was expecting something else, and having made Maureen's acquaintance when she was but two weeks old, you can Rest Assured that I kept my eye on her. You probably think that her last was the most Desperate Measure anybody could possibly think of and even I, I must say, didn't think that she would stoop so low as Perjury and Forgery to attain her Nefarious Ends, and how can one assume responsibility for that which one is too high-minded to suspect. Mother and Father afterwards said that she was too Young and Innocent to know what she was doing. What I say is, if she was so brimming over with Youth and Innocence, why did she continue, in her Under-Handed Way, to answer "What" whenever anyone yelled "Maureen" at her? Why did she accept her Birthday Check for 13 dollars when it was made out to Maureen Stoddard? Why, in short, did she make every attempt to Conceal the Fact that she, our Fourth Girl and Seventh Child, the sister of our Bosom, was in reality no longer Maureen Stoddard, but Mary Queen O. Scots?

Nobody knows exactly how Maureen got the idea of changing her name. Maybe it was when Mr. Moore explained to her after the Post Office business that, as long as her name was Maureen Stoddard, she had to accept letters So Addressed. Maybe it was from one of the dopey kid books she reads. Maybe—and this is a suspicion that will Go With Me to the

Grave—it was from an idea that John insinuated into her mind. I say this not maliciously, but because John's Sense of Humor is so terribly Highly Developed.

The first inkling we had that All was Not as It should Be was one day when Maureen didn't tear upstairs right after breakfast to get at her letters. Instead she went swimming. After lunch she did not tear upstairs either. She went out on her pony. After supper, instead of practicing on the typewriter, she read *Captain Blood*. The next day it was the same, and the next day after that. No more trips to the Post Office to collect the new batch of mail; no more letters, no more typing, no more illegible-handwriting practice. None of us said any-thing, because we thought Maureen had at last conquered her Inner Compulsion. Even I, Intellectually Awake as I am, sus-pected nothing, because, unknown to her, Maureen had been under my Close Supervision since the moment Lieutenant Grant had left the house two weeks before *except*, and this is a large except, for the day she spent in New York with Mother on her fall shopping trip, which being not present, I can Assume no Responsibility for. The mistake I made was in trusting Mother to keep Maureen under equally Close Supervision. But as Mother often says, in her telling way: "A watched pot never boils."

Mr. Moore broke the bad news this time. Mr. Moore was getting pretty tired of Maureen, and who can blame him if he sounded Irritated to a Degree when he talked to Mother over the phone? Mr. Moore said not that he wanted to make trouble for anybody, but did Mr. and Mrs. Stoddard happen to know about the position the United States Post Office had been placed in by their daughter Maureen. And he said that he'd keep on calling her Maureen till his dying day no matter *how* many papers said her legal name was Mary Queen O. Scots.

When Mother finally put down the phone and started to tell us what Mr. Moore said, she was almost Unable to Speak, which is very unusual with Mother. She often suffers from incoherence because of what Father calls Fitful Paralysis of the Speech Organs Due to Overusage (to which Mother says, What can you expect, one decent God-fearing Schultz chained for life to 11 crazy Stoddards). But it is almost unknown for Mother to be Struck Dumb for over thirty seconds at a time, which is what Prepared Us for the Worst.

It seems, Mother told us, that the day after Maureen returned from the shopping trip to New York, she went to the Post Office at nine o'clock as usual, to get the mail. She took out the 89 letters that were addressed to her and brought them up to Mr. Moore at the window.

"I'll thank you to return these to sender, Mr. Moore," she said, in a haughty way. "There is at present no Miss Maureen Stoddard residing in Sheraton, Connecticut."

Mr. Moore, who can be Very Amusing, just stared at her for a minute.

"I see," he said. "Well, if you're not 'residing' here any more, Maureen, maybe you can tell me where you can be reached?"

"You misunderstand my meaning," said Maureen. "The fact is there is no Miss Maureen Stoddard Extant."

"I suppose I'm standing here looking at the Queen of Sheba!" said Mr. Moore.

"No," Maureen snapped, "at Mary Queen O. Scots." And she turned on her heel and walked off. (Maureen practiced Turning on her Heel all one summer and now has it Down to Perfection.) Mr. Moore said he just stood there looking after her and thinking "Getting too big for her breeches, that kid." Little did he know. *Little!*

So the next morning when Maureen came in he had not only the original 89 letters for her but 107 more, which if you are Mathematically Inclined you can easily see adds up to 196, No Small Sum. Mr. Moore said:

"Look here, Maureen, let's you and me stop fooling around

and take these letters home with you. This isn't any metropolitan Post Office, nor yet a Storage House." And Mr. Moore said darned if Maureen didn't go through that spiel she put on yesterday all over again and so did he, except that this time, when she came to saying "Mary Queen O. Scots," she added: "And I can prove it." And with that, Mr. Moore said, she hauled a piece of paper out of her sweater pocket that said all official and legal that hereafter be it known and so forth that Miss Maureen Stoddard was Miss Mary Queen O. Scots. And it was signed and sealed and attested and all the other things by a Judge in New York City.

After the third day, when Mr. Moore had almost three hundred of Maureen's letters cluttering up the Post Office, he telephoned Judge Baker, who is an Attorney-at-Law, and Mr. Moore said darned if Maureen wasn't within her Constitutional Rights in refusing to accept those letters, but he also said darned if he wasn't going to find out if Maureen's Ma and Pa knew about all this Monkey Business.

Mr. Moore was pretty Wrought Up by the time he finished telling Mother all this, and don't think Mother wasn't too, when she finished telling us. I ran down to the kitchen to get her a Coke, which always helps Mother a lot, being Southern, and then I got Maureen from her room, where she was starting *Captain Blood* over again. I escorted her wordlessly to Mother's room, my face Hard and Cold, for anyone who gives up the Fair Name of Stoddard, even for one as Exalted as Mary Queen O. Scots, deserves no sympathy.

No sympathy was exactly what she got. Even John, with his Highly Developed Sense of Humor, and even Matt, who by an Evil Twist of Fate, was not born but only married into Our Family, were shocked. Even so, it was only after Father said if she didn't tell how she did it he would Employ Detectives, that Maureen broke down and confessed. Although I cannot truthfully say that she exactly broke down. It was more like a small crack.

As I had suspected, she accomplished her Coup when she was in New York with Mother, *not*, as I assured everybody several times, when she was in Sheraton with me. Whenever Maureen goes to New York she has to ride on top of the Fifth Avenue bus from Washington Square all the way up Riverside Drive and back again, which, besides costing twenty cents, is a tremendous waste of the time which more Adult minds would wish to spend in the movies. This is one of the many things about which there is no arguing with Maureen. She just simply *has* to, so on this particular day, when it became clear that Maureen could control herself no longer, Mother, who was very busy, decided that she was old enough to go alone, so she put her on the bus and left her. It was then that Maureen Accomplished her Awful Purpose. She got right off the bus at the next stop after Mother couldn't see her any more, went down to the City Hall and had her name changed.

"But, Maureen," Sally said, "How did you know where to go and what to do?"

"Oh, Judge Baker showed me. I told him about that friend of Father's called Uno Hoo, and I said I wanted the application blank for him. Of course, I gave a different address, too, on account of supposing to be a resident of New York."

"Didn't they even ask if you had your parents' permission?" Father broke in. "I must say . . ."

"Oh, yes," Maureen answered. "But I knew they would. So in the place where it said: 'If applicant is a minor, parent or guardian sign here,' I put down your name, Father. You should have seen it," she added, looking conceited. "It looked just *like* your handwriting, Father; you couldn't have told the difference with a *telescope*. Just think, from now on I can sign all your letters and checks for you!"

Father got out of his chair with the most agile leap I have ever seen in a Man of his Years.

"Sally," he said to my Mother, for Mother's name is also Sally, after our eldest sister, "Sally, in all the long and interesting history of the Stoddards, there has never been a case like this. Maureen is obviously a throwback to the Schultzes, and I therefore turn her over to you. Personally, I am going out to send for a list of the less exclusive reformatories."

And he left the room in which can only be described as a Towering Rage. I did too.

So that is why my sister Maureen is at the Convent this fall instead of two years from this fall. As for her Tender Years, Father says she is Old in the Ways of Sin. Her literary genius has not gone unnoticed, however, for her original letter was reprinted as a Prize Winner last week in the International Pen Pals magazine, and 3,240 answers have been forwarded to her, since. But as Father says, that little situation is one the dear Nuns will have to cope with, as Maureen is now their responsibility. I'm certainly glad she is no longer mine, because Do Not Evade Responsibility is the fifth most important thing in our family.

CHAPTER 7

Pastiche

After Aloïse Heath's death her husband Ben asked her sister Priscilla, who had been Aloïse's editor at National Review, to go over her papers. Dismiss any thought of tidily labeled file cabinets, or neatly typewritten manuscripts in looseleaf binders—that was not how Aloïse Heath operated. Pieces of manuscripts and other writing were found in the pocket of the winter overcoat now hanging in the attic, scribbled on the end of a child's math test, running around the edges of a grocery bill, stuffed in a drawer, serving as a book mark, buried in a pile of parking tickets in the glove compartment of her car. They were all demonstrably hers, indited in her distinctive block script, only barely decipherable. The search was long and thorough and the findings were slim and mixed. Some were hopelessly dated, many incomplete, quick sketches for a longer piece she never wrote. Some were extraordinary. One such was "A Letter for Maureen" (Chapter 6), completed but never dispatched to Ladies' Home Journal, which was eager for more of Aloïse's work. Why she made so little effort to have it published we don't know. Other pieces, although incomplete, we reprint in this pastiche because of their stylistic merit and because of what they reveal about ABH. One is "I Am What You Might Call a Salt," a spirited account of a week on Bill Buckley's yacht, The Panic, which, however, never got that meticulous final going-over that made her writing so polished. We reprint here also "The French Have

a Word for It," part of a larger travel section in the (1969) first
edition of Mrs. Major. "The French Have a Word for It" is a
take-off of an enormously popular book of the 1940's, French
without Tears, where the jollies came through a literal translation
of French into English. The other travel pieces, written in 1960
on a trip to Egypt, Jordan, and Israel, are dated and have been
dropped. Before leaving on that 1960 trip to the Holy Land,
ABH wrote a poem to her children, "Prayer to a Guardian
Angel," and left it for them on the bulletin board in the family
pantry. One of the children saved it, and a second poem,
"Thoughts on Surveying a Host of Heaths," which we also reprint.
Also, because it is so revealing of the fun she could make out of
the smallest things in life, we include two notes she left her
undomestic sister Priscilla about various housekeeping deficien-
cies encountered on one of those occasions when Aloïse Heath
took refuge from the hurly-burly of her home in West Hartford
in Priscilla's sunny, quiet New York apartment to finish the
article she had promised National Review ten days earlier. Finally there is a piece—little more than a sketch—but touching
and perceptive, about what President Eisenhower's invitation to
Nikita Khrushchev to visit Washington just three years after the
Soviet invasion of Hungary meant to one young Ukrainian refugee in West Hartford, Connecticut. He couldn't believe it of
his adopted country; neither could Aloïse Heath of her native
country, but she was less surprised . . .

Prayer to a Guardian Angel

Now as I watch my children sleep
My angel, guard their bed.
Inform with innocence the dreams
Inhabiting each head.

When on the morrow I take wing
To soar through thy domain
Assign one wingèd spirit to
My transatlantic plane.

Bless thou the pilgrim and the way
And all this household keep,
Grant me a happy homeward flight
And now—untroubled sleep.

February 10, 1960

I Am What You Might Call a Salt

My brother Bill is a dear boy, but he suffers from a curious ambivalence: though he is profoundly pessimistic about things such as the State of the Union, the encroachments of Communism, and President Kennedy, he is wildly optimistic about the ability of others to conquer time and space. (". . . Well, *that's* no problem: bring the children! It's just a matter of renting ten more camels after all . . .")

I was in Sharon, Connecticut, on Monday and *The Panic*, Bill's boat, was in Edgartown, Massachusetts, a ferry and a taxi away from Wood's Hole. Bill told me Wood's Hole was a leisurely three and a half hours' jaunt from Sharon; actually, driving at high speed, with no stops for lunch or to go to the bathroom, I reached Wood's Hole in only eight hours.

Bill would meet the 3:15 ferry (". . . Oh, easily") at Vineyard Haven ("Well, unless you're planning to take in a double-feature *en route* . . ."). Naturally, I barely made the 8:00 ferry.

Otherwise, Bill would be in the dining room of the Edgartown Yacht Club from 7:00 to 9:00 ("By the furthest stretch of the imagination, you're not coming that late, are you?"). *Naturally*, the taxi from Vineyard Haven to Edgartown dropped me at the Yacht Club at 9:30. The dining room was closed. The office had no idea where, or if, Mr. Buckley was.

Otherwise, Bill would be in the harbor on *The Panic*—sitting in the crow's nest with binoculars and rosary . . .

All I used to know about the sea was "a wet sheet and a flowing sea and the wind that follows fast." I knew that because it was the high point of the year in the Upper Fourth Form's Read-Aloud Period at St. Mary's Convent, South Ascot, Berks. Sister Margaret Mary used to substitute a line of her own composition which went:

"The salt spray and the sea's spume and the breeze that follows fast" on account of the vulgar giggling that historically greeted Masefield's original. Of course the Upper Fourth giggled just as violently at Sister's lines (after all, we'd been waiting all year) (the Lower Fifth told us what to watch for) but I suppose it did limit the class yak's opportunities for general wit and gaiety.

Anyhow, that's how I even knew *that* much about the sea. (Not very interesting, was it?)

Today, I am what you might call a salt, if that's what you call me. (I know the expression is "old" salt, but actually I am in very *early* middle age.)

Besides a wet sheet and a flowing sea and a wind that follows fast, I know: anchor, furl, galley, guy, head, head (there are two meanings to "head" and I know both of them), jib, jibe, keel, port, reef, sheet, spinnaker, starboard, tiller, and a lot of other things that have momentarily slipped my mind. (Actually, I knew anchor before.) What I know best is sheet. A sheet on a boat is not what you thought: it is a rope. On my brother Bill's boat (which is where I learned all these things in only five days) the sheet is my personal rope. (Well, naturally, when I'm on the boat.) I hold the sheet and when people say "Let out the sheet" I let the rope *out* and when they say "Pull in the sheet" I pull it *in*.

Persons who are *not* salts in early middle age are undoubtedly asking themselves why we of the sea don't just say "Let out the rope" and "Pull in the rope."

Aha!

The fact of the matter is that there is *another* rope: (Actually there are several other ropes. Actually there are *millions* of other ropes, but I'm *not* talking about them. The other rope I *am* talking about *is*) the guy. On *The Panic* the guy belongs to my sister Priscilla. Yes, yes, yes, *when* Priscilla's on the boat! Priscilla does to the guy what I do to the sheet (see above). We have to. If we refuse, it's mutiny.

Every other time you pull in and let out ropes the *sheet* becomes the *guy* and vice versa. This is to keep you mentally alert. Priscilla and I are not mentally alert (well, I mean we are mentally alert, but not *that* mentally alert) so we just change places every other time so that I'm always the sheet and she's always the guy, because *it is very important to pull the right rope*. Otherwise the boat *jibes*. Jibe means to go backward or sink or something. Or maybe it blows up: it must be something maximally catastrophic because when you forget whether you are the *sheet* or the *guy*, the men on the boat become hysterical. And repetitive. They say: "The guy, the guy, the guy, the guy" and "Let it out, re*lease*, re*lease*, re*lease*" and when you say, "I heard you, I heard you, I heard you" (acidly), they don't even hear *you*, because they're still gabbling, "Re*lease*." I mean, you'd think your finger was poised over the all-out-nuclear-war button, when you were supposed to be ringing for more ice. Another thing about the *sheet* and the *guy* (are you tired of all these italics? I mean do you think you've really got it? About those ropes? All right): Another thing about the sheet and the guy is that they are on opposite sides of the *cockpit* (I know, I know, but I have to italicize cockpit because if I don't you will naturally assume that I've been talking about airplanes all this time. I mean, if you haven't been concentrating. You *have* been concentrating, haven't you?).

The cockpit on a boat—well, that's not entirely fair.

The cockpit on *Bill's* boat is a sort of three-foot-square inden-tation in the deck with seats around it: to sit on in case the boat goes aground, I guess. Or is becalmed. But the sheet and the guy being on opposite sides of the cockpit means that Priscilla and I are on opposite sides of the cockpit. This proxim-ity is what insurance companies call a "continuing hazard": not to *The Panic*, but to us. (One night, Bill, who is known as a card, roguishly twinkled, "It's not your proximity, it's your presence that's a hazard.")

Another thing to know is whenever they say: "Whose turn for breakfast (lunch, dinner)?" on *The Panic* it is Priscilla's and my turn. If we refuse, it is not mutiny, but what it is, is peanut butter, bacon, jelly and mayonnaise sandwiches. Grilled.

The Panic has two bunks below (you don't say below *what* on boats, you just say below) and a triangular closet with a triangular bed on which you sleep triangularly so as to free a great deal of valuable space to store garments in. And, after all, you don't need all that space between your feet when you're lying down, now do you? The triangular closet is called the "owner's cabin" which is a real tribute to the chivalry of boat-owners.

Another thing is: you say "boat" not "ship." I mean *we* say boats, we salts that is. And when we get home we tell my son Buckley, who is not passing Ben the pepper, that where the pepper is, is on the windward reach of his port elbow. That's where. Idiot.

Two Notes Left in Priscilla's Apartment After a Frustrating Visit

I. If I had to leave a philodendrum,
   To Priscilla I would never lendrum
   For between Priscilla and philadendra
   The *entente* is *cordiale* but hardly tendra

II. Soap makes things clean
    Soap makes dishes clean
    Clean dishes are *nice*.

    President Johnson likes clean dishes.
    Mrs. Kennedy likes clean dishes.
    God likes clean dishes.

    Clorox is not soap.
    Air freshener is not soap.
    E-Z Off Oven Cleaner is not soap.
    Johnson Wax'N Klean is not soap.
    Leprechaun Leather Mist is not soap.

    Your dishes have
    Been washed with
    Helena Rubinstein's
    Deep Skin Cleanser

    (To hide soap is worse)

The French Have a Word for It

Every now and then I take a little trip with the only people in the world who don't care whether they pull into Avignon by five o'clock sharp or a quarter past twelve—all of whom are my mother and my sisters. Since there are seven of us, all easily nauseated, it only takes a minute or two for anyone who is sick, sick, sick of it all to whip up a few traveling companions.

Our traveling plans are not quite as casual as this would seem to imply. Although we very seldom arrive at a given destination when we thought we might, we never for a moment lose sight of where it was we were heading for. Thus, when Priscilla and I left Paris at two o'clock one afternoon headed for Rouen, 79 miles away—we *got* there. Maybe because of the fact that we left Paris by the wrong *porte* and found our-selves launched in new, unplanned and fascinating territory—we didn't get there until four days later, but we got there. If you can envisage the maps of France and Spain adorned with a broad, swooping, felt-tip red line, advancing with purposeful-ness and grace from Paris up to Normandy, east and north to the tip of Brittany, and down again toward the Loire country and, eventually, the Pyrenees and Spain—and then if you can envisage that intelligent, cultured red band crisscrossed, zigged and zagged, and occasionally encircled by a squiggly black thread-line—well, the red band was our tour, and the black line was our trip. We saw a lot we didn't plan to see, but we didn't miss anything we *had* planned to see.

When I get back from my journeyings, my husband, Ben Heath, who knows good and well he couldn't *pack* enough tranquilizers to last him through a trip with me, kisses me tenderly, gazes fondly into my eyes, and says: "My, travel *is* broadening, isn't it?" (Ben's peripheral vision covers an amaz-ingly wide range, his oculist says.) Naturally, I always pretend

I think this observation is based on the mirror of my soul (I should be the one to say: "I can always lose weight on my own meals"? And have him say: "I know"?), so all the way from Idlewild to downtown New York I tell him things about Delphi or Luxor or Tel Aviv which turn out to be things that wouldn't necessarily have broadened other people.

I didn't bother with all that when I came back from France last month. When I got the travel-is-so-broadening deal, I simply said: "What will you? In France, the paste-of-fat-liver on the host-table only, makes the life in rose worth the pain." I remembered just in time that the Gallic shrug this kind of conversation calls for would almost certainly split my coat seams, but, as it turned out, my Gallic shrug was unnecessary—Ben had already changed the subject.

I speak French in English quite often now. You have no idea what a conversation-stopper it is if you want a conversation stopped.

No one, I'm sure, really thinks that French people go around saying: "L'état, c'est moi," or "Vive la différence," or even "Sonnez les matines" all the time; but I sometimes wonder whether Americans know what French people do go around saying all the time? Actually, I don't wonder: I've made up my mind: they don't and I'm going to tell them. For one thing, the French go around asking people to put *essence* into the gas tank of their car, which doesn't sound very rational, does it? And when they want to hear the six o'clock news, do they turn on the radio like normal people? Not at all. They put on their telephone-without-wire. And in the towns where they're having anti-noise campaigns you know what they tell drivers? They tell them they are prohibited to functionate their sonic notifiers. The French aversion to loud sounds can be a matter of exquisite delicacy as illustrated by the advice in a book on etiquette discovered by my brother John, age 12, at the Château de St. Firmin where we spent the summer the year Maureen was born. It recommended use of a music box in the bathroom to drown out "les chutes sonores et gazouillement orageux de la toilette" ("the sonorous rushes of water and tempestuous warbling of the toilet").

Another thing—and this is terribly important in terms of Psychological Significance—when you fill out a questionnaire in France (every four hours) you know what you're to write under "Occupation" if you're a housewife? You write: "Without." *That*, of course, is just a little more Continental than a red-blooded American can get; and unless French question-nairists undergo a radical change of attitude, Mrs. Benjamin Wild Heath will spend no more francs in France—not even her sisters'. The next time I go I'll use my maiden name.

I do not accuse the French of saying:

"I love thee, I adore thee,
What devil dost thou want again?"

all the time, because they don't. That's what Americans say all the time. I began to notice the linguistic idiosyncrasies with one of my sisters. My French has always been good (well, let's face it: superb), but Priscilla's is so absolutely dashing that before we'd been in Paris a full day I took two verbal paces to her rear and stayed there till we got back home.

What shook me was that, two hours after we arrived, when a waiter asked us what we wanted to drink, Priscilla answered "Two seriouses," and he brought us each a large glass of beer,* which was exactly what we wanted to drink. (I could have ordered two large glasses of beer, all right, but you know what I would have had to ask for to get them? . . . Exactly.) So the next morning, when Priscilla told the hairdresser to give me a "shampooing" (this is a French noun which rhymes with "Rond Point") (well, *naturally*, "Rond Point" in French!) and

---

* And that's just about enough of all those middle-class snobberies I can see running through your head. We were eating *choucroute garnie*, and when you eat *choucroute garnie* you drink beer, whether you're in Paris or Milwaukee.

a put-in-pleats (*mis-en-plis*) I didn't get a bit nervous (and actually, they didn't put my hair in pleats; they gave me that same nice set I always get at Schultz's, Thursdays at ten) but I did get interested in French semantics. I mean, when I see madness, I look for method; and when you ask for a serious and get a glass of beer, or ask for a put-in-pleats and get your hair set—well, in West Hartford we call that madness.

The very first time I was able to put my finger on this method was the very first time we were in an elevator that stopped dead between the *rez-de-chaussée* and the *sous-sol*. In accordance with our different levels of sophistication, I cried: "To the help!," which is what you cry when you are trapped in an Alpine pass in a blizzard at midnight and wolves are attacking you; and Priscilla shouted "The ascendor does not march," which means that the elevator isn't working. After a while we stopped for a cigarette and we noticed the sign on the door. "By means of the telephonic apparatus which finds itself at the interior of the ascendor, *ladies*," the sign said pointedly, "and *gentlemen* may inform the concierge in all calm that a mechanical anomaly has passed itself." There is more to this message than meets the eye, we found. And you will find, too, if you try to say "anomalie mécanique" when not in all calm.

French elevator companies, which are more sinning than sinned against, I'm sure, maintain order by imposing certain standards of labial agility. French railways, which are probably the opposite, use psychological tactics to maintain gentlemanly standards in their clientele. The railways instill in their passengers a dark and crawling fear of the unknown.

Anywhere in the world, as anyone in the world knows, if you're caught trying to hitch a free ride on a train, you get thrown off. As the "New Haven" puts it: "Passengers without tickets will be ejected." In other words, when you ride the "New Haven" you know exactly where you stand—which is along the tracks, about two miles north of Meriden, if worse comes to worst. But where do you stand if worse comes to worst on a French train? They don't tell you. What they do tell you would translate literally as: "Persons in transit who are discovered to be without tickets of passage will find them-selves in a position of the greatest irregularity." But what is the penalty for finding oneself in that position? Exile? Prison? Torture? Being put in a cage and hung from the ceiling of a dungeon for seven years like that twelfth-century bishop? You just don't know! Only persons who *have* found themselves in a greatly irregular position know—and *they* aren't talking! But you don't go gallivanting around France without train tickets, either!

There is plenty of Gallic subtlety in their journalism, too. Have you ever noticed that French people buy six or seven newspapers a day? No? Well, I really don't care whether you have or not. The fact is, they do; and the reason they do is that they are constantly, desperately, vainly trying to find out what on earth *finally* happened. In France, Priscilla and I were forced to conclude, newspapers increase their circulation not only by reporting, but also by ceasing to report.

Take the case that opened with six-inch headlines last October:

ALL FRANCE SEIZED BY HORROR
*The Small Hermione, Aged But of 8 Years
Accompanied by Uni-Legged Sadist, Vanishes!*

For a few days there was no, but no other news in any paper. Priscilla and I, hourly glued to the daily paper, learned a good deal more about the historical background of the uni-legged sadist (the *life* that man had *led!*) and less about that of the Chateaux of the Loire than we intended when we planned our trip. But one morning, at last, we read that a gay party of *pique-nique* had encountered the ravisher, self-poniarded in a

park. A note nearby stated forcefully that the ravisher's personal preference was for a French Algeria, and that the small
Hermione was, as once again the French translates literally,
"habiting the home of his brother's married daughter."

Priscilla and I were greatly relieved to hear the good news
about Hermione (we have a tenderness for small girls aged
but of eight years), but since neither of us has been brought
up to take the word of uni-legged sadists, especially those with
his record, the next morning we bought another paper, just to
check. There was nothing about the small Hermione in *Le
Matin*, so we bought *France-Soir*. Nothing in *France-Soir*, so
we bought *Le Figaro*; and *l'Aurore*, and *l'Humanité*, and *La
Croix*. And pretty soon we were buying six or seven papers a
day, just like everyone else in France. Because by the time we
realized that we'd never, never find out whether Hermione
really *was* at the ravisher's brother's married daughter's, we
were trapped again. We absolutely *had* to find out what happened to the rest of the mutilated lady of Bethune, 42.3 kilograms of whom had been recovered from various parts of the
river, and 20.07 kilograms of whom the police had carelessly
allowed to slip through their fingers, according to the coroner,
who estimated that, fully integrated, there had been 63 kilos
of her—minimum.

To be sure, a vacation devoted to elevated linguistic studies,
as ours was, *does* prolong one's readjustment to everyday life;
there's no question of that. Just a few minutes ago, for instance,
I found myself telling Buckley Heath that I happened to know
it was he, not Chrissie Bailey-Gates, whose apple-fling "bruised
the oriental window" of my bedroom, a not very idiomatic
way of complaining about a broken window facing east. And
I understand that only last week, Priscilla gave the janitor at
National Review her "parole of honor" as managing editor,
that *NR*'s personnel are "defended absolutely to discard foreign
bodies into the water closet"—which mystified a janitor who

wanted only to be assured that refuse was not permitted into the toilet.

And I can hardly wait for Thanksgiving. "Sacred Blue!" I am planning to say to Ben. "There is already a quarter hour that I have demanded you to segregate the turkey!"

It Takes All Kinds
(1959)

Connecticut history is studded with the names of men who risked death and disgrace in the cause of freedom: Ethan Allen, Nathan Hale, Oliver Wolcott, Daniel Webster, John Brown, Bronson Alcott, and five signatories of the Declaration of Independence are only a random sample. Our capital city adopted the world's first written constitution—in 1639—and so informs the trespassing traveler by means of tasteful, upper-class-type signs, which mention, *en passant*, the fact that he is at the portals of

HARTFORD, CONNECTICUT
HERE WAS BORN SELF-GOVERNMENT
BASED ON CONSTITUTIONAL FREEDOM

Stephen Boychuk, formerly of the Ukraine, now of Hartford, Connecticut (the very same), where he works as a reviewer for the Phoenix Fire Insurance Co., learned the history of his new home along with its language; for here, one finds, "they tell you all the time in language school about Charter Oak and Thomas Hooker and Rochambeau and say to watch parades of Governor's Footguards, first commander Nathan Hale, which was guarding George Washington, Father of our Country, with the same uniforms as now and how old Connecticut people was brave people that made even wars to be free." He came to know our tongue and fell in love with our past, but apparently it had never occurred to him that the lives of the Founding Fathers were naturally more stirring to their descen-dants than were the lives of, say, Stephen Boychuk's mother, father, and three young brothers—which turned out to be so *short*, for one thing. And when he did find out, he simply didn't *adjust*.

When Khrushchev's invitation to visit the United States in September 1959 was announced as an irrevocable fact, young Boychuk waited, respectfully to be sure, but expectantly, for his seniors, the "born-Americans," to formulate a protest in which he could join. He allowed himself four days during which the lonely voice of Senator Thomas Dodd, echoing from the rafters of a deserted Senate, sank soundlessly into the back pages of the Nation's Oldest Daily Paper, which is Tom Dodd's home-town paper—and Stephen Boychuk's, the *Hartford Courant*.

At the end of the four days ("Is, at the end, ninety-six hours. Long time, when you are waiting, waiting") he called a meeting of the "foreign-borns," the Estonians, the Hungarians, the Lat-vians, Lithuanians, Poles, and his own countrymen, the Ukrai-nians, at which they plotted an anti-Khrushchev rally of their own. Boychuk became president of the organizing committee and Robert Kuttner, a Ph.D. attached to Hartford's famous Institute of Living, became its secretary. There were no other officers, nor did anyone remember to give the organization a title. "We were too busy for officers and committees and names. At the meeting they say: 'Who to ask the City for place; who to write to newspapers; who to paint signs, find speakers, give money . . .'"

Mr. Boychuk wrote the City Manager asking for permission to hold a meeting in Bushnell Park, which faces the State

Capitol. The City Manager was deeply shocked. "Dear Mr. Boychuk," he wrote, gritting his teeth, "I have discussed with your secretary the problem which this presents to the city. The President of the United States has asked us all to avoid any embarrassment to the official visitor to this country, Nikita Khrushchev. Under the circumstances, I tried to convince . . ."

(The members of the committee didn't really want to embarrass Khrushchev either, of course. On the whole, they would have preferred to kill him. But then the committee's "circumstances" are the twenty thousand graves they left behind, and the City Manager's was a Presidential Request. You can see how hard it was for everybody to get together over this thing.)

The letter continued: "The actual permit must be granted by the Director of Parks. Therefore, I am forwarding your letter to him with my reply, with the understanding that if he grants such a permit, it will be for the use of Colt Park at 3:30 P.M . . ."

There are ten major parks in the City of Hartford. Nine of them are carefully landscaped lawns, bright with the season's flowers, shaded by Connecticut's great elms. One of them, in the shabby "South End," is a weedy field bright with beer cans and bubble-gum wrappers, shaded by the backs of nineteenth-century factories and abandoned warehouses. . . . The committee, with many thanks, refused the City's kind offer of Colt Park. (It was when he was apprised of this refusal that the Director of Parks referred to Robert Kuttner and his organization as "you subversives"—but only in a burst of what turned out to be amnesiac indignation.)

The City, however, ignored the refusal and announced to the newspapers that the committee would hold a rally in Colt Park from 3:30 to 4:30 P.M., Saturday, September 17. Only the City, and only the committee knew, as the saying goes, "different."

But there was a viper in Hartford's official bosom, and the

viper struck. Stephen Boychuk was informed, through clandes-
tine sources, that the tiny half-circle of Bushnell Park immediately in front of the Capitol steps belongs not to the City,
but to the State—and the State of Connecticut, less concerned
with the niceties of hospitality, unhesitatingly gave Boychuk
permission to use its strip of land. The rally proceeded as
scheduled, on September 17, and, as requested, in Bushnell
Park. What *agonies* of embarrassment Mr. Khrushchev must
have gone through when he heard!

Of course, only five hundred of the two thousand they
expected attended the rally, but that's not counting the people
who assembled in Colt Park, stood around for a while, and
drifted away. No native American organization was represented, but then no native American organization in Hartford
considered the demonstration in the best interests of the country. At least 25 native American *individuals* were there, however. (It takes all kinds.) Some other people might have turned
up, but the City had detailed a small army of policemen to
help the audience distinguish State from City property, and,
from the back, the rally might easily have been mistaken for a
police convention. (One middle-aged woman, after ascertaining
the boundary line, stepped over into enemy territory and looked
nervously at the nearest policeman. But he only looked nervously away—he turned out to be one Officer Zavkrantsky—so
the woman stepped back, rather relieved, on the whole.)

Nobody heard the speakers very well because, around four
o'clock, the Governor's Footguards had a parade around the
Capitol grounds and then held a band concert on the city side
of Bushnell Park (Rochambeau Day). The sky was blue and
the sun was shining; the Footguards wore the bright uniforms
they wore when "was guarding George Washington, Father
of our Country," and the sober young East Europeans in their
rented black suits stood quietly on the Capitol steps, holding
their home-made signs and gazing over the heads of the crowd

at the pageant of America's past. Overhead, the Capitol flags whipped and snapped in the breeze. On Connecticut's flag, when the angle was right, you could make out our State Motto: *Qui Transtulit, Sustinet* (Those who come to us from abroad will nourish our state).

Thoughts on Surveying a Host of Heaths

I wandered lonely as a cloud
That floats on high; o'er vale and hill
When all at once I saw a crowd
A host, of Heaths—it chills me still.
Beside the lake, beneath the trees
A tremor seized me in the knees.

Continuous as the stars that shine
And twinkle on the Milky Way
They stretched in never-ending line.
I would not wrench my eyes away.
To house them one would need a ranch
To feed them—Lord, it made me blanch.

The noise that issued from this gang
Reverberated over me.
I clapped my hands o'er ears that rang
And damned the jocund company.
I gazed—and gazed—but little thought
What wealth to me the show had brought.

For oft, when on my couch I lie
In vacant or in pensive mood
They flash upon my inward eye
And then I bless my solitude;
Reach for my pencil and my scroll
And write anew on birth control.

CHAPTER 8

How to Raise Money in the Ivy League

The *very first issue of* National Review *(November 19, 1955) carried a piece by Aloïse Buckley Heath, "How I Raised Money for the Ivy League," the story of what had happened a year earlier when she addressed a letter to 27,000 alumnae of Smith College suggesting that before contributing further to the annual college fund appeal they might want to inquire why five professors who supported Communist-front organizations were on the staff. This was during the McCarthyite wave of terror—and the witch hunt was on . . . but not for the professors.*

Some morning last month, each of several million Americans refilled his coffee cup, lit his second cigarette and opened, without enthusiasm, a letter from his Alma Mater.

"Dear Fellow-Grad," the letter probably began. "Do you realize that our contributions account for 80 per cent of ALL THE SCHOLARSHIPS our college offers to deserving high school students?" Or perhaps: "Did you know that our Physics Building has long been OVERCROWDED, UNDEREQUIPPED and in desperate need of a STUDENT SMOKING ROOM?" If the letter came from a woman's college, it almost certainly asked: "Do you remember: the October gold of the elm by College Hall; the faint blue haze from the piles of leaves burning on Appletree

Lane? Can you still hear the twilight sound of the college carillon? We hate to intrude Need on Nostalgia but ... HOW MUCH ARE YOUR MEMORIES WORTH TO YOU? "

Each of several million Americans stopped reading right there, reminding himself to remind himself to send $10 (if a man) or $5 (if a woman) to the Best College in the World. A lot of them even will.

Several thousand Alumni Fund presidents, who have been hoping, this year at least, for $25 (from a man) or $10 (from a woman) will, upon receipt of Fellow-Grad's check, weep and wail and gnash their teeth and consign to outer darkness this latest of a long series of appeals that failed.

All, however, may not be lost; the Class Goal may yet be met. For to any university—and the chances are doubled in the Ivy League—may come the unbelievable stroke of good luck which smote Smith College in the spring of 1954: the stroke which broke all previous records of alumnae contribu-tions.

The day the gods smiled on Smith was the day a number of her graduates received a letter from me. The letter was three paragraphs long and, even as other fund-raising letters, dealt with conditions at Alma Mater. The response to my letter (and I shall present documented evidence) was not simply electric— it was atomic. According to the Spring 1954 issue of the *Smith Alumnae Quarterly*:

In the ten days following February 25 [the day my letter was received] both the President's Office and the Alumnae House were inundated with letters, telegrams and telephone calls from Alumnae. Many of the letters included checks ranging from $1.00 to $1,000. A goodly proportion came from alumnae who had already contributed to the Alumnae Fund this year, and a considerable number from alumnae who had never before contributed in any way to the College. Several letters and checks were sent by men whose alumnae wives during their lifetime had been contributors.

And this was only the beginning. A Hartford newspaper reported that the town of Northampton had had to assign extra postmen to the college, and that students were being pressed into service as clerks in the treasurer's office to handle the deluge of cash, checks, and, presumably, old family silver which arrived every quarter hour on the quarter hour from loyal Smith alumnae. In less than three months, the world's largest women's college received more money than had ever been collected in any full year in its history.

The year 1954—God help us all—some day may be known as the year of the $64,000 question. Like the television program, the letter I wrote to the Alumnae of Smith College revolved around a single question; but my question, even unanswered, turned out to be worth almost four times as much as Hal March's. My question concerned not student scholarships, not faculty salaries, not university equipment, not even Bright College Years. My question concerned the documented Communist-front affiliations of specified Smith faculty members who help form the opinions of two thousand young minds every year; two thousand young minds which come to college eager, open, and, for the most part, blank. "Wine maketh merry, but money answereth all things." The alumnae of Smith College, with or without the influence of wine, answered my letter with two hundred and eighty-four thousand, eight hundred and thirteen dollars, plus twenty-four cents. An answer from the college administration was never given to and, in fact, was never requested nor required by almost 28,000 of the certified educated women of the United States.*

To College Treasurers, Alumni Contributions Chairmen, American Universities, Inc., and all other professional or amateur fund-raising organizations, I offer the secret of my

---

* For some reason, Smith does not include in her take for 1954 the donation referred to by the alumna who wrote me that "to affirm our faith in Smith College, my mother ('22) has just contributed $500,000 for a new dormitory."

success. The process is simple and the fruits are sweet. The formula: *Point to Pink Professors*. The immediate effect (to write as colorfully as possible) is that the administration turns purple and the alumni see red, but in a matter of days the tumult and the shouting die under the cool green whisper of thousands of dollar bills.

The letter which, to Smith, was worth roughly $2,000 a word was described in its full horror by the *Smith Quarterly*:

The letter began "Dear Alumna." It suggested that contributions to causes or institutions implied moral responsibility on the part of the donors. It questioned whether contributors to Smith wished to "sponsor the employment of men and women who, through their teaching positions, may be influencing young minds in a direction contrary to the philosophical principles in which most of us believe." The letter then named five members of the Smith faculty who, "to-gether with other members . . . have been or are presently associated with many organizations cited as Communist or Communist-front by the Attorney General of the United States and the Committee on Un-American Activities." The letter concluded with the suggest-ion that the alumna who could not conscientiously help to make the employment of such teachers possible should withhold contributions "until the Smith Administration explains its educational policy to her personal satisfaction."

In one small matter, the *Quarterly* misquoted me. I began my letter, not "Dear Alumna," but "Dear Fellow Alumna," and the word "fellow" was not to be sneered at in terms of its cash value to Smith College. "To be addressed by you as a 'fellow alumna' makes me so ashamed I am doubling my con-tribution," one of my correspondents informed me. "I had hope-fully supposed," hopefully supposed another woman, "that to warrant the title of 'a Smith alumna' one must cherish the principles of intellectual freedom, due process [sic] and indi-vidual integrity. I have today forwarded a check . . ." Among hundreds of unsolicited donors was one who, referring to my letter, asked reproachfully: "If the graduates of an independent liberal arts college do not know better, who does?" (The question is hazy, but the answer, I think, is clearly people who are not graduates of an independent liberal arts college.)

A spokesman for the sensitive-soul group wrote that she was increasing her contribution though "never again will I hold my head quite so proudly, knowing that you are, indeed, a 'fellow alumna.'" This reference to posture, incidentally, was repeated so frequently and in so many variations that I can only conclude it has become a nationwide mark of recognition. In any large congregation of women, look around: those with heads un-bloody but bowed are Smith graduates.

The success of the *Point to Pink Professors* technique in fund-raising is, then, demonstrably enhanced if the Pointer is a graduate of the college in question. To find such a Pointer is of course difficult but, even in the Ivy League, not impossible. President Wright of Smith College openly admitted that among his 28,000 alumnae there were a disloyal two who had asked for the basis of the information I offered.

The "Shame on You" reaction, however, is only one approach to an indignant alumnus's pocketbook. According to my files— and I am sure it is unnecessary to state that my 'phone lines, telegraph operator, and postmen were just as busy as Smith's— there is also an inordinately large and vocal minority which belongs to what might be called the Nausea, or Pepto-Bismol School. This group expresses displeasure not only by bowing its head, but by losing its breakfast in the process. Folding money seems to be used by the sorority as an alkalizing agent. "Your insinuations are nauseous," one woman wrote greenly; "I shall contribute *heavily* to Smith College." Another increased her donation because "your shameful behavior towards Smith College frankly turns my stomach." And again: "Your outrageous letter made me ill—literally ill . . . sending $100 over and above . . . "

Let it not be thought, however, that the P. to P. P. technique institutes only an emotional or physical reaction in the average college graduate. Larger by far and even more fluent, though perhaps not quite so rich, was the group which, after reading my letter, contributed to Smith for intellectual reasons. Upon hearing that their money helped to pay teachers who, according to the government of the United States, had pro-Communist records, the Intellectuals rushed in a body to the bank.

"My loyalty to the College and my faith in its officers are stimulated *as never before*; I am sending today a check doubling my largest previous contribution," wrote one. A 1929 graduate, who described herself as a "student, member of the Administrative staff for three years, and currently member of the Board of Directors of the Alumnae Association," informed me that "your letter has deepened my loyalty to the College *more than any single event* I could have imagined." (And yet, earthquake, fire, and flood are, conceivably, not beyond the scope of her imagination.)

Another intellectual-type note disclosed the fact that "although I know only one of the faculty members you mentioned, I judge [apparently from the information I had offered] that all of them are very good teachers who can stimulate the students at Smith College." One of many "duplicate check" senders owes to me the decision that her Alma Mater is Great. "Because," as she pithily put it, "it is always the great institutions of learning that are attacked first in any police state, for the colleges harbor the 'dangerous' people, the people who know how to think, whose minds are free." (One of the extra little rays of sunshine in my campaign was the fact that I enabled Smith's President to reach the same conclusion. "If I ever had any doubts about the vitality of the liberal tradition in Smith College," he confided to the student body, ". . . they have been resolved. . . . These letters have indicated to me that in the past Smith College has been a very great liberal college."

It was in this same speech that the President announced triumphantly that only two of 28,000 alumnae, trained to search for truth with a liberal's curiosity, had asked for the basis of what he called "these vague charges and insinuations."

Others of the Bluestocking Group—all of whom have a real gift for words—sent contributions to Smith College in defense of "the American tradition," "the brotherhood of man," "academic freedom," and "the Christian way of life." All of these attributes being clearly embodied in five little professors—four-fifths of an attribute per.

I should like to state at this point that, in the interest of academic accuracy, I have ruthlessly excluded from my Intellectual Group even the most fluent of the one hundred and ten ladies who expressed their "confidence" in Smith College. I have also excluded a high-minded and wealthy graduate who declared that "Senator McCarthy would have *profited* from the education I *received* at Smith."

Pointing to Pink Professors does not, appearances to the contrary notwithstanding, invariably arouse hostility to the Pointer on the part of the Pointee. In some Pointees (even the one who described herself as "not Catholic or Jewish or anything else subversive") my letter aroused a spirit of Christian charity. Several expressed pity for my "tortured, twisted mind"; several excused me on the ground that I was a frustrated female ("You, madam, are a frustrated female!"); many urged me to place myself and my family in the hands of a good psychiatrist, and one asked if I had "tried God."

And then there were the thank-you notes. "I have doubled my usual contribution . . . thank you for spurring me on," wrote a member of the class of '93. "You have inadvertently done Smith a great favor," admitted an undergraduate. "There has never been so much money contributed as this year," wrote a grateful lady who, in the circumstances, can hardly have been sincere when she added: "Oh, dear, it would have been so nice if only you had gone to Vassar."

Even as mold gave rise to penicillin, one particular letter developed Heath's Law of Fund-Raising. "Dear Mrs. Heath," ran this billet-doux, "Congratulations on your novel (if unethical) method of raising money for our Alumnae Fund. The funds are pouring in, thanks to your letter. Next year you might think up another Smear-Smith stunt to aid the Fund."

Punchdrunk as I was, this letter snapped into focus the whole Smith episode. Derogatory information about Smith equals Smear-Smith equals unprecedented financial support for Smith. If, this year, Smith College were to double its quota of faculty members whose extracurricular activities figured prominently on the Attorney General's Communist-front list, I could, by pointing out these associations, institute another "Smear-Smith" campaign which would double even the 1954 record of alumnae contributions. If Smith tripled its quota, the alumnae would presumably triple theirs.

Although I cannot claim to know what makes the Ivy League graduate tick, I feel I can present incontrovertible evidence as to what makes him give; and my formula, which cannot but constitute a valuable addition to the psychology of merchandising, I here offer without mental or financial reservation. To *Point to Pink Professors* is to institute an alumni reaction as predictable as pushing the bellybutton of a mamma doll—except that in Ivy League alumni, the eructation takes the form of cash.

The late Mrs. Thomas Lamont gave a million dollars to Smith and her son Corliss* to Columbia. Any fundraiser with a keen eye for potentialities can see that Columbia may easily have got the best of the bargain.

---

*A renowned fellow-traveler.

CHAPTER 9

Ladies' Month in the Slicks

*A*nxious to sign up ABH as a regular correspondent, National Review proposed, early in 1956, that she undertake to review different genres of magazines. She liked the idea, in fact she relished the assignment. She had over the years spent long, boring intervals waiting for children in dentists', doctors', and principals' waiting rooms, reading what was proffered: women's magazines. They were called the Slicks in the pre-Helen Gurley Brown era, or, in low-brow offices, movie magazines. In "Ladies' Month in the Slicks," ABH takes a jaundiced look at the inanities of the average woman's magazine, and in "Prosiness in Purple" (Chapter 17), pokes fun at the "they're-home-folk-just-like-you-and-me" pretensions of film stars such as Marilyn Monroe and Elvis Presley, rendered in the saccharine prose of the silver screen press.

A month spent with the Journals that offer the American Woman Companionship in her Home—and this is as long a way to spend a month as I know of—can leave no shred of doubt that the most fortunate, the most blessed of the creatures of the earth are American men. For while American women have security, steam irons, children, mink coats, well-adjusted sex lives, the vote, and color television, they also have the

American man. American men, on the other hand, have security, the benefit of steam irons, children, the prestige of mink
coats, well-adjusted sex-lives, the vote, color television, and
also the American woman. This is the origin of the phrase "all
this and heaven too."

No one, of course, will claim that *all* American women live
up at *all* times to *all* the standards set by the magazines devoted
to them. Some of us, for instance, are no longer 24. (All of us,
though, look ten years younger than our age, thanks to the
October 1956 publication of "Look Ten Years Younger Than
Your Age"—which caused some pretty peculiar situations
among those of us who *are* 24.) Nevertheless, if any skeptical
male doubts that the standards of the American woman are
unbelievably high, one can only conclude that his wife confines
her reading to *National Review*—unless, of course, she just
doesn't *care*. In either case, she will almost certainly flunk this
month's test in one of the most widely read periodicals: "ASK
YOURSELF: Am I Becoming Less Appealing?" Even if she doesn't
"eat too much and become overweight," "neglect hair, nails,
grooming unless going out," or "delay him when he is due at
work," she may not, unless she reads the magazines she's meant
to, realize the dangerous lessening of appeal of the woman
who "makes long social telephone calls," "usually stays up late
at night," or "talks more loudly than her husband." (In certain
isolated circumstances, of course, a "Yes" answer to the last
question would be justified: chronic laryngitis on the part of
her husband, for instance; or the case of a man who might be
worried about *his* Becoming Less Appealing, and therefore refused to talk more loudly than his wife at the identical moment
that his wife refused to talk more loudly than her husband.
We can all see where *this* sort of situation would end, I am
sure.)

The American Man, insensitive clod that he is, may glance
through this month's slick magazines without seeing the word

"husband" or "man" in the table of contents, and assume therefore that these publications are not all about him. The fact of
the matter is, he is so accustomed to the complete attention
and fulsome praise of his women that one periodical this month
had to think up an entirely new angle on "How to Compliment
a Man." For instance: "'What handsome cuff links! Are they
part of a collection?' convinces him he's a connoisseur." Also:
"'I'm crazy about your waistcoat. I wish George weren't so
timid about anything new' appeals to his pioneer spirit." And:
"'That jacket hangs perfectly, but I suppose that's because of
your shoulders' will do wonders for his morale."

Another morale booster for the American man is the fact
that, of 13 love stories, 11 romantic heroes are described as
being "on the stocky side" and that out of a total of 115
different features, 33 are devoted to food. (And if he doesn't
see the connection, his wife does: not only do we have to stay
in love with you when you're fat, we even have to *fall* in love
with you when you're fat.)

Articles about food, then, are articles about men, but the
true woman's home journal does not countenance food in mere
bulk. It must also be simple and delicious. One magazine this
month brings the American woman advice from Mrs. Cooper,
"wife of the former ambassador to India." "'Keep the food
simple and delicious,' recommends Mrs. John Sherman Cooper.
'Let everything about your entertaining reflect your own personal tastes and you can't really go very far wrong.'" Food for
the American man must also be *interesting*: "For a variation
this year, try the ancient custom of baking a mince-pie manger
in a pan ordinarily used for loaf cakes. If you are particularly
handy with decorating, you could make a sugar or icing replica
of the Child to place in the center of the pie." (And the more
whimsical families could allow the children to draw straws for
the privilege of eating the Child.)

Food must also be sheerly pretty: "For sheer prettiness, make a miniature holly wreath to float on top of your Christmas punch bowl"; and the setting is almost as important: "A Christmas tablecloth is an idea an imaginative family votes for . . . As holiday guests linger over coffee, each is given a soft pencil to autograph the cloth, and the hostess plans to embroider the signatures with her new zigzag sewing attachment." (If some of the lingering guests don't have zigzag handwritings, there is always the new Palmer method sewing attachment—though this is not as decorative, to be sure.)

Most gratifying of all, our magazines realize that the American woman is *intelligent* about food. Her husband, who probably takes for granted simple deliciousness and sheer prettiness, will glow with pride when he hears his little wife casually mention to the President of the First National Bank that the tradition of a holiday punch bowl began "at least 1,000 years ago in medieval England. The accompanying greeting, 'waes hael,' meaning 'be well,' established the name for the beverage, and probably was the forerunner of our greeting, 'Merry Christmas.'" (On second thought, she'd better keep that one for her second-grader. "Waes Hael" probably being the forerunner of our greeting "Merry Christmas" is pretty much of a cliché, after all.)

Since we're on the subject of Christmas, it might be well to mention the fact that if anyone in God's country finds the same tired old ties, stockings, and blocks under the tree this year, it can only be because the donor has been lax in her reading this month. The woman who has done her homework will give "GIFTS YOU CAN'T BUY IN A STORE." To the "Tired Businessman" she will give "a paid-up course at a gymnasium for fitness exercises." To the "Harried Housewife" will go "a paid-up course at a charm school or reducing-exercise salon; or a course of paid-up massages or facials; or a paid-for new permanent wave." (This gift had better be limited to harried housewives you know very well indeed.) To a "Young Family" there is almost no limit to the things the imaginative woman can give. For instance: "A storage wall in their house—these require 2 feet of space in a room." (It is especially thoughtful to include a new house large enough to contain new rooms large enough to contain new storage walls.) Or the Young Family could be given "a portrait of the children—it can be painted from a photograph by a good artist." (This brings up a good general rule: *never* have a good portrait painted by a bad artist.) "A set of humorous laundry bags." (Humorous laundry bags are laundry bags with humor.)

Other recommended gifts are certain records which have very recently been issued. One is the "Sounds of Nature," of which the magazine says, "some are more continually exciting than others—the more familiar sounds, such as thunderstorms, or the cackling of a hen." Another record is called "The Sounds of Medicine" and it is "by all odds, the most exciting of the series," even more so, I guess, than thunderstorms and hens. One side records an operation for the removal of a cyst from the neck of a twenty-month-old baby. "The other side, nearly as interesting, presents sounds of various body organs—anything from heart and lungs to an empty stomach—along with a narration identifying the sounds." The magazine adds: "And surely, they're *the* perfect gift for the man who has everything." (Better make sure, first, that he *does* have everything.)

Many an American man reading this far will snort in his unpleasant way: "Ha! Charm, cooking, buying presents! Pretty soft, if you ask me!" Well, in the first place, who asked him? Certainly not I—I'm not even speaking to him. But if I *were*, I should have to point out that the American woman is not only the ministering angel of the male, she is also the guardian angel of his offspring—an indubitably tiresome section of humanity whose main characteristic is the inheritance of all the trying qualities of its paternal progenitors. First of all, the American woman has *lots* of children—or if she hasn't now, she will, beginning in September 1967, for she has just learned that "large families are the happiest, a six-year-old University of Pennsylvania study indicates. Living in a large family emphasizes the importance of the group rather than the individual; conformity is valued above self-expression." (And what real American woman wants to bring up an individualistic creep?) She is also about to eliminate thumb-sucking in the American child, since she reads this month that "a simple way to stop children from sucking their thumbs is suggested by Dr. Clifford L. Whitman of Columbia University to the American Association of Orthodontists. If a child is taught to whistle, he will have to take his thumb out of his mouth." (Some cynics may point out that if he won't take his thumb out of his mouth, he can't be taught to whistle; this is the kind of criticism known as "niggling.")

The American woman has also read "Look, Mom, I'm Dancing" and is about to teach her toddlers grace and rhythm. She will hold dancing classes for preschoolers at which "The singing of nursery rhymes with gestures can top off the session. Their gestures won't be refined, but who cares? *Think* what fun they will have falling down like Humpty Dumpty!" (She might also think, right now, what to do about the little boy who will, during the fall-down-like-Humpty-Dumpty business, point to the shyest little girl in the class and state in carrying tones: "I see Paris, I see France, I see Katie's underpants.")

And with what *spirit* is the American woman imbuing her children this month? Well, with the Christmas spirit. In the first place—"We Think the Most Amusing, Most Sentimental Presents are the Ones You Make Yourself"—she and the children are making the most amusing, most sentimental presents you can possibly imagine out of the ordinary, everyday things we all have lying around the house: 102 Popsicle sticks, for instance, or 89 empty spools; all those old guitar strings and the drawerful of scarlet ostrich feathers. She is also acquainting her children with the real meaning of Christmas—"Your Child and the REAL MEANING OF CHRISTMAS"—by telling them (in a Jewish family) all about the Nativity and (in a Christian family) all about Hanukkah. And if the family is neither Jewish nor Christian? "You may thoughtfully and sincerely have decided that church is not for you. In that case it can hardly have real meaning for your children."

How-true-how-true. If her children seem disinclined to extend Christmas "good will" to Russia, the American Mother can bring an "informed understanding" of the "Communist point of view." For instance: "Are there certain hopes that we truly share with them? A peaceful world, a better day for the poor and oppressed—these are the expressed purposes of Communism." And of Christ, of course.

Do women's magazines encourage their readers to think, though? to probe, to analyze, to venture toward ever new intellectual horizons? They most certainly *do*! This very month there is an article called "Can We Make It Safe to Be Free?" The author concludes that there is no freedom without freedom from security programs; which may not be exactly new, of course, but it's pretty darn probing. He also says that Martin Dies was *worse* than Joe McCarthy. Now there's a brand-new intellectual horizon for you. The more conservative woman may reject any suggestion that there is something worse than Senator McCarthy—but, at least, she has been made to *think*.

Eleanor Roosevelt's question-and-answer column is another thought-provoker. Just one of her answers this month demands far more intellectual analysis than I am afraid many of us have the time for, so near to Christmas. "QUESTION: I know Adlai Stevenson and other important people have belonged to the Unitarian Church, but to me a Christian religion that does not admit the divinity of Christ just isn't a religion. ANSWER: My husband's mother was brought up a Unitarian and later became an Episcopalian, but there never was any question that she was a good Christian. The Trinity is not essential evidently to leading a Christian life, nor does it seem to detract from the reverence in which Christ is held."

How does the American woman accomplish all she does and still remain so young, beautiful, graceful, glowing, and serene, the American woman wonders? By following instructions, that's how. Is she "TIRED AND TENSE?" Or are you, by the way? "Rest and relax wherever and whenever you can. In the bus, close your eyes and slowly open them several times. In the restroom kick off your shoes, pull out your stockings and wiggle your toes. Sitting at the counter put your hands in your lap on your purse, let your head and shoulders slump forward, then slowly pull your ribs away from your waist, straighten up with head erect." There are not nearly so many epileptics sitting around at counters as some people suppose. Most of them are perfectly normal American women resting and relaxing wherever and whenever they can.

When I get *real* rested and relaxed, I'm going to make another stab at something I just can't seem to get the hang of. In one of the stories this month there was a *very* moving love scene in the course of which a woman stood "with her hands clasped on Loren's neck, her red hair pressed against his chin, her lips ardently uplifted." The trouble is, when *I* clasp *my* hands on my husband's neck, press my interestingly graying hair against his chin, and ardently uplift *my* lips, all *I* get is a mouthful of Adam's apple. Don't worry, though. I'll figure it out yet. That's the American woman in me.

CHAPTER 10

Seven Keys to Anomie

'S'*even Keys to Anomie" was commissioned by National Review in December 1956 right after Adlai Stevenson's second unsuccessful presidential bid, a loss that left American liberals in the doldrums: The country persisted in not living up to their expectations. In "Seven Keys to Anomie," ABH dissects the liberal psyche by taking the test, "How to tell if you are an intellectual?", devised by journalist-sociologist Malcolm Cowley. (For the benefit of younger readers: Norman Thomas was a perennial Socialist presidential candidate in the Forties and Fifties, and hence, supremely intellectual.)*

"Who are the Intellectuals?" Malcolm Cowley asked the readers of the *New Republic* at some length a couple of weeks ago [January 1957]. Who are the "freely speculating minds," he inquired, with the disciplined urgency of a man who suspects that unless he finds out he may shortly be reduced to talking to himself.

He knows *what* intellectuals are, all right: they are distinguished from other people by "a special *attitude*"; they are persons "open to ideas"; they also "differ among themselves on every conceivable issue."

He knows what intellectuals do, too, on at least some things. One thing intellectuals do, says Mr. Cowley, is nominate Adlai Stevenson for the presidency. (Which, for my money, means that intellectuals think Adlai Stevenson is an inconceivable issue, and I think so too.) Another thing Mr. Cowley says intellectuals do is, in 1943, as Roosevelt's lieutenants, successfully apply "the ideas of John Maynard Keynes, which after twenty years have also been accepted by many of the leading Republicans"—accepted not, one assumes, because the leading Republicans are intellectuals, but because "the intellectual commonplaces of one generation become the political commonplaces of another."

In the "intellectual community" whose personnel Mr. Cowley seeks, there is, he says, "a division of function." There are those who "expound" and there are those who "willingly listen" (and I anticipate with considerable pleasure a follow-up article in the *New Republic* to be entitled: "Who are the Intellectuals Who Willingly Listen?"). "Note," Mr. Cowley continues, inaccurately, I fear, "that the two roles may be exchanged. Professor Smith, who has been suggesting a new American policy in the Middle East, steps down from the platform and listens while Professor Robinson expounds the Dead Sea Scrolls; then Robinson listens in turn while Professor Braun develops a new theory of city planning." Anybody who reads this paragraph carefully can see the flaw in Mr. Cowley's illustration. Professor Robinson actually is *not* a "willing listener"; he only listens to the others so that they will listen to him, and you can see his point, because, frankly, Professor Smith and Professor Braun don't know beans about the Middle East or city planning. (I really don't know why Mr. Cowley even mentioned those three. Simply everybody calls them the Scratch-My-Back Club.)

I hope that nothing I have said suggests that Mr. Cowley is indulging in a rhetorical question when he asks, "Who Are the Intellectuals?" Conservatives, as we all know, positively wallow in what is known as non-constructive criticism, but no liberal would feel qualified to voice a dislike of your blueberry pie unless he could suggest an extra 2 tbs. shortening and perhaps a little less sugar; nor would Mr. Cowley ask who the intellectuals are unless he knew how to find out.

The social psychologists, who have been working on the authoritarian personality and "what they call anomie, some-times defined as a state of indifference resulting from blank discouragement," are just the boys to spot all those faceless intellectuals. Mr. Cowley suggests that they be identified by means of seven questions (supplied by himself), the answers to which would be graded by comparison with a list of "typi-cally intellectual answers to the questions." The typically intel-lectual answers which characterize typical intellectuals would, I assume, be established by a preliminary canvassing of the people who nominated Adlai Stevenson and of Roosevelt's lieutenants in 1934.

For any readers who are interested in making Cowley's Intel-lectual Register, I herewith present his questionnaire, along with a list of typically intellectual answers, which I just happen to know because I just happen to be typically intellectual, even if Mr. Cowley doesn't know who I am.

1. "*What are your degrees, from which colleges or univer-sities?*"

Don't worry about the degree on this one; anything from B.A. on up will do, unless your degree is in science, in which case you must have a Ph.D., and it must be in physics. Your college is the real test here; the only acceptable alma mater is either: a) a private college or university in the East, *or* b) a state university in the Middle or Far West, *or* c) the University of Grenoble, but NEVER d) *any* college or *any* university *any-where* in the Southern half of the United States unless you are William Faulkner (and I don't think you are).

2. "*Whom did you vote for in the last two Presidential Elec-tions?*"

Intellectuals diverge widely on this one, so you can be pretty much on your own. Any one of the following four answers is

correct: a) Adlai Stevenson, Adlai Stevenson; b) Adlai Stevenson, Norman Thomas; c) Norman Thomas, Adlai Stevenson;
d) Norman Thomas, Norman Thomas. (Actually, if you want
to go into the nuances of the thing, in 1956 Norman Thomas
was less intellectual than in 1952 and Eisenhower had become
much, much more intellectual, but let's not take any chances.)

3. *"Do you often read any of the following magazines?"*

Simply check any magazine with a circulation of 25,000 or
under except *National Review*. After *National Review*, write:
"???" or "!!!" Either is acceptable.

4. *"If you drive a car, what is the make and how old is it?"*

The typically intellectual car is a) if expensive, old, or b) if
new, inexpensive. If you are fool enough to answer, "Cadillac,
1957" you will almost certainly flunk; a 1929 Rolls Royce, on
the other hand, is perhaps the *most* in intellectual cars and may
easily net you a 20-point bonus.

5. *"Do you spend much time looking at TV?"*

If you think you've passed all the other questions, it might
be safe to branch out into a little whimsy here. In any case,
the following answers, personality-geared, are all good:
a) "Never"—straight-type intellectual; b) "Only Milton Berle"
—droll-type intellectual; c) "Any soap opera"—sarcastic-type
intellectual. If you have *any doubts at all* about the other
questions, however, give the first, or straight-type answer.

6. *"Do you believe that the United States should continue
testing hydrogen bombs?"*

Here again, any one of three answers rates maximum score:
a) "Absolutely not!"; b) "Certainly not!"; c) "No." (*Now* are
you beginning to see why it's so difficult to pinpoint intellectuals?) You should firmly resist the temptation here to say:
"No, but . . ." or "No. However . . ." This kind of garrulity is
almost as unintellectual as saying Yes.

7. *"Which of these attitudes toward racial segregation is closest
to your own? [with an appended choice of opinions]."*

Ignore all those choices of opinions, which are simply traps. Write diagonally across the list, in very large black letters: "UNDER NO CIRCUMSTANCES!!!" and then underline it twice. This is a highly typically-intellectual solution to the problem and it saves thinking about all those choices, which is so time-consuming.

There! Test's over! That wasn't so bad, now was it? And if you remembered everything I told you, you're in!

"The passing grade," Mr. Cowley reassures us, "would be 70 or 80, not 90 or 100; for intellectuals differ among themselves on every conceivable issue." And when you think of all those different colleges and cars, you can see his point.

CHAPTER 11

The Sociology
of the Carpool

The average mother of private-school children drives 191.7 miles a week.

Her average drive covers a distance of 4.9 miles.

She gets in and out of the car 191.7 divided by 4.9 multiplied by two times a week, which I am too tired to work out right now.

Her hips are 2.3 inches broader than those of the average mother of public-school children.

She may easily drop dead in the flower of her early middle forties.

These statistics have been privately compiled.

The main difference between private and public schools is not what you think (though they are that, to be sure; and getting more so every year); it is that public-school children are taken to school and brought home by bus instead of by Mother.

Public-school children are also taken to Afternoons with Mark Twain by Hal Holbrook, to Band, to dental check-ups, Driver Education, eye examinations, opera dress-rehearsals, Manual Training, movies, museums, music lessons, puppet shows, sewing, singing, symphony concerts, tutoring, and typing, which are curriculum enrichments, by bus; except when the bus brings the enrichments to the enrichees.

Private-school children, who have been sitting at their desks all this time doing long divisions, are enriched after school at places their mothers drive them to and drive them back from.

(This is not necessary; it is because women don't like their children to run around whistling *Chopsticks* through gaps in their green teeth while every other child on the street is trilling *La Donna è Mobile* through braces. In Italian.)

What this can mean for the mother of a basic family of five is a daily driving schedule such as: 8 A.M.—Jim and John to Kingswood; 8:15—Pam and Priscilla to Renbrook; 8:45—Timothy to St. Joseph's Nursery School; 12 P.M.—pick up Timothy; 3 P.M.—pick up Priscilla; 4:30—pick up John; 4:40—pick up Pam; 5:30—pick up Jim.

Catechism is on Monday from 3:45 to 4:45. On Tuesday Priscilla goes to dancing-school from 4:30 to 5:30 and Pam has a piano lesson from 5 to 6. Wednesday is the day Timothy goes back to school from 2 to 4 for Nature, and John has his braces checked. It is also the day Jim plays in a Kingswood "game." If the game is away, you pick him up whenever he gets back to school. If it is a home game you have to go and watch him. He gets off the bench three times: once while you're picking up Timothy, once while you're picking up Pam and once while you're at the dentist with John. On Wednesday Pam goes to dancing-school from 7 to 8:30.

Well! I'm sure you're as anxious not to read about the rest of this week as I am not to write about it, and I don't blame you: there's not a word of truth in the last two paragraphs. Actually, you drive Jim's schedule every fourth week, Pam's every seventh week, John's and Priscilla's every Friday and Timothy's on alternate Tuesdays and Thursdays—all because of a magnificent institution called the *Carpool* (and I was beginning to think I'd never get to it, weren't you?).

The carpool is one of the ten most important institutions of this century; that is why it is one word, not two, which Webster's New Interplanetary will confirm. No woman in her right mind would send her children to a private school if she had to do all that driving, and if she weren't, her housekeeper wouldn't do all that driving either. What it boils down to, as you can easily see—or you can if you concentrate—is that without carpools, private schools would cease to exist; public schools would be in a state of pandemonium, what with having to take in all those private-school children; and that this nation would have to appraise candidly the possibility of the Central Congolese getting to Mars before us. That is why the carpool is one of our ten most important institutions, which you didn't believe the first time I told you.

Carpools are undemocratic, exclusive, authoritarian and efficient. They are composed of reliable, prompt, emotionally stable women with loud voices, and of women who pretend that they are too, with loud voices.

The kind of pool which involves the least mileage and the most mental stress is formed by women who watch birth announcements for six months before and after their own babies are born, and who have the conveniently located candidates for St. Joseph's Nursery School spotted and signed up before they're a year old. Participating members are annually reinvited, and losses to other schools or to fathers who have been transferred to Cincinnati are annually replenished—usually no later than April of the preceding year. Typed schedules are circulated early in August, and are not alphabetical but *fair*: if Brown gets a short week at Thanksgiving, Washington's Birthday is assigned to Whitmore; and no member has an extra tour of duty just because there are 37 weeks in the school year, six women in the carpool and she married a man called Aabijian.

In any neighborhood, this is the carpool which has the firmest hold on the most mothers of the fewest children in the smallest area—and if you don't mind phoning Stevie Shipley's mother twice a week to find out if he ever did pass his entrance exams for Pomfret, you may be the first on the waiting list for his place in next year's pool. However, unless you know for a fact that no one else is checking with Mrs. Shipley four times a week, you might as well look around a little.

A carpool, after all, has only one *raison d'être*: to drive as seldom as is necessary to get your own children to school and back every day. Simple as this sounds, it can involve the most intricate mathematical calculations—the less you want to drive, of course, the more intricately do you mathematically calculate.

Is your problem a fourth-grader, for instance? Then a cursory glance at the average height and weight chart in the 1962 Almanac will prove to you that 14 grammar-school children are physically crammable into one station wagon. Unless you are paying attention you will not learn that the Sixth Grade girls will tell you all year long how "squeezed" they are; and that they are also bigger than the Almanac admits and than you. What you have to decide—before, not after the pool begins—is how you really and truly feel about Sixth Grade girls. (Are you emotionally stable? Can you pretend you are?) Should you settle for 12 children and peace and quiet or should you hold out for 14 and listen to *remarks* all year?

Well: which can you bear least: Sixth Grade girls or driving?

Don't underestimate the importance of finding out.

Now that you have decided on a 12-child pool, you have to proceed to the consideration of the relative advantages of carpooling with large or small families. If you join the 12 children of five mothers you'll draw every fifth turn, but you won't have so many stops to make or so far to drive between them. If, on the other hand, you comb the state for the 12 children of 12 mothers, you will only drive one-twelfth of the time, but it will be all over God's green earth. You'll have to start out by seven at the very latest, you realize, and what with all the traffic in the afternoon you'll be lucky to get home by five. What you have to decide right now is whether you're the sort of person who operates best under conditions of mild unhappiness every fifth week or of acute misery every twelfth week. And what about the eleventh week ... could you keep from brooding ... brooding ... ?

Once you have decided on the five-mother pool you will realize that it has still another advantage: it is much the easiest to remember if you're sensible enough to organize it by days. You simply gear yourself to driving every Friday of the foreseeable future. That's not too hard—mentally, I mean—is it? (Incidentally, when I say Friday, that's what I mean. Friday gives you the day after Thanksgiving, Good Friday, the first day of Christmas and spring vacation. Actually, I've had a good deal of luck with "no-school" snowstorms on Fridays, but that *could* be coincidence.)

More or fewer than five mothers should not organize a pool on a daily basis if they have me in it. I only mention me because my name is Legion. Last year I was in a four-man pool in which each of us drove one day a week plus one extra day every fourth week. My extra day occurred—psychologically, you understand; not chronologically—at such erratically varying intervals that I spent the better part of the year calling for boys when I wasn't supposed to or going back to bed with the coffeepot when I was. It is not the sidelong glances that you get right here when that happens; it is the difficulty of keeping your pajamas from slipping back down your ankles while you assure Peter that of *course* you didn't forget—you were just getting into the car when he phoned; or of persuading Mark that you knew all along it was Mrs. Driscoll's turn: you happened to be out driving and you thought he might like a lift. (Actually, I sometimes wonder whether that group didn't *suspect*. I mean, doesn't it seem a little funny that every one of those boys got a car for his sixteenth birthday?)

When you have several different carpools—as who hasn't?—overlaps can pose some pretty sticky problems to those who have forgotten to anticipate them. You can only get away once with not being able to imagine why all those taxis you ordered didn't turn up. After that your line has to be that you think it's just a blast to pick up six boys, five lacrosse sticks and a left-over pair of skis at Kingswood and hurtle across town fast enough to collect the seven Renbrook girls only 15 minutes late. "It's just like playing Sardines, isn't it?" you cry gaily all the way home. The silence remains stony, but at least they can't tell their mothers Mrs. Heath forgot again.

A lateness of over half an hour, though, especially in the winter time, when you drive up to find your little group huddled and forlorn in the bleak darkness of an empty schoolyard, is heartbreaking. There's nothing you wouldn't do to make it up to them—like a stop at the Friendly for a round of Awful-awfuls. Awful-awfuls cost fifty cents apiece, it turns out, and by the time the children have finished them and you have paid for them, they may think you're not so bad after all, but you think you're worse.

The more usual purpose of treats is not the propitiation of children but the ensurance of their good behavior. In September, treats are almost always graham crackers or ginger snaps, but they tend to become more and more elaborate as the year wears on and every women hears of the absolutely yummy things she is the only mother who never brings. (A carpool which has reached the chocolate eclair stage by Christmas, on the other hand, has clearly lost its head.) It is important to observe the rules of common sense in this quest for yumminess: the woman who brings Fudgsicles to her three o'clock the day she has the 4:30 dancing-school pool will have to wash out the entire inside of the car with soap and water between 3:30 and 4 and will have only herself to curse. Another good rule is never to bring bottles of soda pop and straws to an all-boy pool—not even on the hottest day—because they suck the soda up into the straws and squirt it at passing cars. This is the kind of thing you need your loud voice for.

On the whole, though, it's best not to pay too much attention to what goes on in the back seat—unless they're squirting soda pop at you, of course. In that case you simply roar: "Roger Davis, would you like to walk the rest of the way home?" (The time he said "Yes," though, and I made him get out in the middle of the snowstorm, I honestly did not know he had a fractured ankle until I saw the crutch sticking out of the snowbank where the other boys had thrown it.) If they start throwing books at each other, it is best to park the car on the side of the road and exhibit emotional stability until they've stopped. Even this is unnecessary if the books are being thrown by Fourth, Fifth or Sixth Form boys. Their aim is invariably excellent, and you are in no danger whatsoever.

Occasionally there may be stationed on one of your carpool routes a policeman who does not like it when a child sticks his head out of the car and shouts: "What's old pennies made of?" and all the others shriek "*Dirty Copper!*" At least he doesn't like it twice a day for nine months of the year, which is when the children like it. If this should be the case, humor him. I myself find that the easiest thing to do is to work out a detour around him, though I understand some mothers made the children stop it.

But what fun it all is, actually—these hours we spend in the midst of lively, eager children, with their innocence, their gaiety, the sudden, short-lived tears . . . Ask any woman; nothing, *nothing* but a chauffeur could part us from our carpools.

CHAPTER 12

The True Sprit of Chrismas

After overhearing some of her offspring discuss the United Nations' Bill of Rights for Children, which they had been given as a class assignment, ABH drew them out on the subject and produced what would become the first of a series of eight Christmas pieces. "The True Sprit of Chrismas" was published in National Review in 1959.

Many persons our ages of 12, 10, 8, 6 think the sprit of Chrismas is about toys and presents instead of about the real sprit. These persons are inmature and childless. As will be seen.

Today at Assembly, everybody got a copy and got read to, the UN Declaration of the Rights of the Child, which turned out it was the Chrismas present from the United Nations to all the children in the world, also which Pam, 12, and John, 10, have to write down about constructively and Priscilla, 8, and Buckley, 6, be prepared to explane in there own words by Monday. This is our free-thinking thoughts, for nothing is black and white but gray.

The first part, before the Principles start, is very oratory and good except for punctuation (commas not periods after paragraphs) and reptitous (absolutely 5 paragraphs in a row begin with "Whereas"). Persons that are always tearing down, tearing down would probbly mock this instead of saying the United

Nations did pretty good, spelling the long words this composition is absolutely full of.

PRINCIPLE 1: *All children shall be entitled to these rights,
without distinction or discrimination on account of race, color,
sex, language, religion, political or other opinion, property, birth
or other status, whether of himself or of his family.* Those who
think will easily see that who their talking about is none other
but the U.S. of America (world smelting pot), for in other
countries from us (Europe, England, Russia, Wildest Africa,
etc. etc. etc.) there isn't enough different population from the
main to do discrimination at. (Except by inmost feelings, hard
to wipe out, unforch.)

Why do they drag in sex, one asks ourself? Because the
United Nations regard sex purely, like dictionaries, where sex
is if you are a boy or a girl (you can look it up)—not the reason
children are not allowed to see practicly every movie in the
whole world. It is a well-none fact that most parents comitt
discrimination on children by sex (by wether they are male sex
or female sex, other words.) Ex:—: Sataday mornings, boys
(M. sex) have to clean out cars in a ice-cold subzero gerage,
wile girls (F. sex) only have to vacume warm & cozy carpets.
And yet again about color (something meening race, but they
already said race in this PRINCIPLE so they now meen color).
Why? Because, Ex:—: Some persons, who dirt shows on more
than other persons because of there snow white color are all
the time getting it in the neck (like parents saying: "Good God,
your angkles"!! venial sin) when that happens to be the exact
night one washed *with soap!* All this shall end.

One thing the United Nations forgot:—: discrimination by
age, like:—Ex.:—In 2 years, could Pam, now age 12 drive a
car in S. Carolina? Yes!! In Conn.? No!! Could Jim, our
brother of 14 marry Linda who he loves in India? Yes!! In
Conn.? No!! Showing that the UN forgot the main thing

the child get's discriminated for. BUT: after all: nobodies perfect:

PRINCIPLE 2 (really getting going): *The child shall enjoy special protection and shall be given opportunities and facilities, by law and by other means, to enable him to develop physically, mentally, morally, spiritually and socially in a healthy and normal manner and in conditions of freedom and dignity.* Their going to start some laws, and unless quite a few parents wise up, we happen to know quite a few parents (including by marrage) that will end up incarserated. Because when the UN finds out, surely soon, that every single child in the world spends absolutely the best years of his life from infantry to adultery sitting on a hard seat, bending his head over books that is rooning his eyes and with the most absolutely boaring stuff poaring, poaring, poaring into his ears. At the same time when they breathe *in* constantly sniffing germs of namonia, chicken pocks, nefritus so they practicly only dare breathe *out* (practicly impossible):— all of which contrary to health and freedom:—then the UN will edict that this situation must CEASE!

PRINCIPLE 3: *The child shall be entitled from his birth to a name and a nationality.* This is also in the Sprit of Chrismas because it portects children from being called Blooper and Kiki even when big, which can become absolutely humalating. Ex:— When John was born our brother Jim was 4 (dificult age) and Jim liked our Uncle Reid so he absolutely made every one call John "Uncle Reid" after him (Uncle Reid). Funny then, but how would John feel nowadays if Mrs. McLeod said in class: "Uncle Reid, suppose you take the next passage?" Like a fool. Principle 3 also portects people from the fate of Philip Nolan, who had to live on boats and not have a nationality for having got mad at the Government once, tho not till grown-up. But children's fate, through the passage of years is to become grown-up or else dead. So look before you leap, which the UN does.

PRINCIPLE 4: *The child shall enjoy the benefits of social security. He shall be entitled to grow up and develop in health; to this end special care and protection shall be provided both to him and to his mother, including adequate prenatal and postnatal care.* This sounds like mostly for Mothers, but think, think, just exactly where would children be without prenatal Mothers? NOWHERE. And prenatal Fathers are not so absolutely necessary. The First Nowell would have been in a sanidary, recently-modernized hospital if people had only had the UN then. The Massacre of the Holy Innocents would be absolutely an object of forbiddance and mortal sin, under penalty of the law.

PRINCIPLE 5: *The child who is physically, mentally or socially handicapped shall be given the special treatment, education and care required by his particular condition.* In the intersts of the questioning mind, one has to admit that this principle is hard: because:—"physically handicapped" means crippled and those children, they say, have to go to special schools for crippled children:—"mentally handicapped" means retarded, and those children have to go to special schools for retarded children:—"socially handicapped" means Negro in the South but, as is well-known, those children have to come *out* of special schools for Negro children in the South. Does that make sense for physicals and mentals to go *in* yet for socials to come *out*? Not that who are we to critisise, never less, may be grown-ups should clarify there thinking on the topic.

PRINCIPLE 6: *The child for the full and harmonious development of his personality, needs love and understanding. He shall, wherever possible, grow up in the care and under the responsibility of his parents, and in any case in an atmosphere of affection and of moral and material security. Payment of state and other assistance toward the maintenance of children of large families is desirable.* This one may seem to say a lot of things one already knew, like "love and understanding," etc.etc.etc., but the important thing after all, is that it is still on the side of children, other words: sprit of Chrismas. One may well ask ourself, although, about assisting (paying) people of large families (personally in our favor), which if they do, they have to make there mind up about populations exploding. For, besides the joys of parenthood, if you get paid too, where will it all end?

PRINCIPLE 7: *The child shall be given an education which will promote his general culture and enable him on a basis of equal opportunity to develop his abilities. The child shall have full opportunity for play and recreation, which shall be directed to the same purposes as education.* It is hard to see how the UN missed the things wrong in this, unless there wrist was getting tired from writting. *Wrong thing No. A:*—There absolutely just isn't anything equal in people's opportunity to learn culture that would be general. Like in West Hartford, U.S.A., culture is French, Mythology, Music, Hiawatha, and things like that, but in Wildest Africa culture is Hunting lions, Shrinking heads, Building huts of clay and wattles made, and things like that, none of which there is any of in West Hartford. (Even if their was some way this could be arranged, it would not be very fair to Wildest Africa children.) *Wrong thing No. B:*—(the part about play and recreation). Unforch, as even the dumbest know, play and recreation that is directed always turns out into one thing:—RELAY RACES.

PRINCIPLE 8: *The child shall in all circumstances be among the first to receive protection and relief.* Vere dignum et justum est (altar boy's joke by John). Others, except priests, look it up.

PRINCIPLE 9: *The child shall be protected against all forms of neglect, cruelty and exploitation. He shall not be the subject of traffic in any form.* (It is a known fact that sometimes children run right strate across *without* looking *both* ways. Think: nothing is black and white: all is gray.) Next part: *The child shall not be admitted to employment before an appropriate minimum age.* This is one of the most absolutely Sprit of Chrismaslike things the UN ever said in its life. For NOTE:—Employment means working for *money.* How far far worse indeed, therefore, is the involatary slavitude children have to do Satadays, not only for *no* money, but not getting their riteful allowance if they don't. This also shall be changed by law.

PRINCIPLE 10: *The child shall be brought up in a spirit of understanding, tolerance, friendship among peoples, peace and universal brotherhood, in full consciousness that his energy and talents should be devoted to the service of his fellow men.* These sweet and nobble words show how the Uniteds have even *improved* the Sprit of Chrismas. For in olden days, you were supposed to love your fellow men (even the ones you couldn't stand) yet use your energy and talents for you and yours, which you had to, the world being such a mess. In our day, you only have to have a sprit of tolerance, friendship, etc. etc. etc., and even that you only have amons peopleS, much more practical than among peoplE, if you get our meaning (see letters we put in capitals.) Also, the new laws of the Governments of the UN will take care of like nutrition, housing and other postnatal care of you and yours, so there will be nothing left to do *except* be devoted to the service of your fellow men.

Thus we see, the UN Declaration of Rights of the Child is the true sprit of Chrismas, and also cinchy.

—Composed by Pamela, John, Priscilla and, sometimes, Buckley Heath.

Typed by their mother.

CHAPTER 13

A Housewife Looks at Soap Opera

In 1945 Aloïse Heath was living in a tiny house in Falls Church, Virginia, with her husband, Ben, a major in the Army Air Corps working at the Pentagon, and her son Jimmy, a little over one year old. Ben drove to work in the morning, leaving Aloïse, carless, at home with the baby, to cope with housework, diapers, baby formulas, rationing, shopping—and loneliness. One distraction was the radio, and she found solace, as did millions of other young American women in like situations, in radio soap opera. One wasn't meant to like soap opera, one was, after all, a Smith graduate. But ABH did. She wrote down why she did, and sent her piece off to Ladies' Home Journal in New York. A few days later, a Mr. Kahler—a most excited Mr. Kahler, who identified himself as a senior editor of Ladies' Home Journal—called her to say they were buying the piece, that they would pay her $500 for it (FIVE HUNDRED DOLLARS), and did she have any more? Aloïse Heath thought it was a joke; it took all of Mr. Kahler's resources to persuade her that he was who he said he was, that he was serious about buying "A Housewife Looks at Soap Opera," and that he wanted more from her. It was the first piece she had ever written for publication, she explained. Was Mr. Kahler sure he was sure? He was.

If Doctor Gallup will be kind enough to lend me his facilities for a few weeks, I should very much like to take a Heath poll on the blazing question of radio soap opera. My poll will be exclusively devoted to the reactions of that lowly creature, the housewife, who is concerned neither with the future of radio nor with the insults to her intelligence with which soap opera is said to abound, but merely with one question—not world-shaking, certainly, but not unimportant: Can "The Road of Life" be turned high enough on the kitchen radio to be heard while she makes the beds?

For the housewife, I notice with pride in my sex, has not joined the swelling chorus of recriminations heaped on soap opera by those whom it is not intended to please. The housewife, if only by that silence so becoming to a woman, is demonstrating her complete and lasting loyalty to the only form of entertainment possible during the pursuit of a career which gives one more mental leisure than any other career in the world—housework.

When I was six and a rather backward pupil at the Sacred Heart Convent in New York, Sister Felicity used to reprove me for beginning sentences with: "I don't think." This was an error not so much of grammar, she maintained, as of logic. One can think *not*; one cannot *not* think.

Twenty years later, still backward, perhaps, but no longer at the convent, I found myself musing a great deal on Sister Felicity's thesis, principally in an effort to prove her wrong. Of course, I was unsuccessful; it is impossible not to think. But how heavenly to be able to turn off one's mind like the proverbial faucet and go blankly about the many daily activities of a woman which require utter mindlessness.

The intellectual side of the housewife's day consists of innumerable such decisions as: there is, or is not, enough soap in the dishwasher; the cake is, or is not, done; the baby's new formula does, or does not, agree with him. But unfortunately, these do not keep busy even the housewife's mind—and that mind must be kept filled for roughly 14 hours every day.

Our day—or at least my day, which is not just about the same thing, but exactly the same thing—is not a maiden's dream. (I concede that I am slower, clumsier, and generally unhandier than almost any other housewife not congenitally idiotic or semiparalytic; but on the other hand, almost any other woman has a lazier husband and standards immeasurably higher.) We arise a few minutes before six o'clock, summoned in most urgent fashion by a small human alarm clock in the next room. From then till nine-thirty is occupied with feeding and changing the baby, cooking and eating breakfast, washing and drying the dishes, making the beds, tidying the bedrooms. From nine-thirty till eleven we bathe, dress and feed the baby again—more heartily this time—and put him out in his carriage for the long sleep the book says he will be ready for. Now we are free, free for the one profound, pressing problem of the day, one on which we can bring all the forces of our intellect to bear: shall we first 1) wash the diapers so that they can dry in the sunny part of the day, 2) make the baby's formula while we're still one bottle ahead of ourselves, or 3) clean the house, just in case anyone, be it only the laundryman, should drop in and notice its laissez-faire, not to say chaotic, state? We decide haphazardly on the formula, with the result that 1) our diapers are still damp when we take them off the line at five o'clock and we spend our evening at the ironing board, and 2) not only the laundryman, but our mother's oldest friend, gets an eyeful of our living room, and our reputation as a housewife, shaky at its best, becomes a cherished memory.

When the bottles are sterilized and the formula made, it is a quarter past twelve. When the diapers and other baby clothes are washed, it is one-forty-five. The baby's next meal is due at two, so with a sandwich or an apple in one hand, we make culinary motions with the other. It is now, please note, two o'clock in the afternoon. We have worked an eight-hour day. All there is left is housecleaning, marketing, cooking dinner, feeding the baby, washing the dishes, tidying up the kitchen, and then ho! for the mending basket till ten o'clock when the baby gets his final feeding of the day and we crawl into bed beside our husband, who is sleeping the imperturbable sleep of one who has spent eight grueling hours at a desk.

This lengthy and tedious description of a housewife's day I relay in all its depressing detail to emphasize that every 24 hours (and I mean *every* 24 hours; Sundays and holidays are worse; Christmas and New Year's unrelieved nightmares) the housewife has, for 14 hours, work on her hands and nothing on her mind.

The solution, obviously, is to get something on her mind. The question is, what?

There are two types of roughly every human being, even housewives, and these are, among other classifications, the so-called intellectual—those who had one or more years of college and read *War and Peace* during the Nazi invasion of Russia—and the non-intellectual, or those who did not. Another, and perhaps fairer, way of making this classification would be to say that some people, when they are alone, must have a book in their hands; others require a piece of needlework. *Omnium humanum in duo partes divisum est*: readers and potterers.

For our purposes we shall make the terms "intellectuals" and "readers" interchangeable, because, though not in all, in the majority of cases they are. The intellectuals, then—or readers— are, I regret to say, those who, in spite of a widely prevailing fiction to the contrary, are the least able to fall back on the resources of their own minds. They not only crave, they *require* outside stimuli. The non-intellectuals, or potterers, are those who have no such requirements, who are able to ruminate gently, peacefully and in silence for hours at a time.

I refer you on this point to any of several hundred articles on Mr. and Mrs. America, with their pleasant evening picture of mother knitting by the lamp in the living room, and father pottering in his tool shop in the basement. Father and mother can work with their hands so happily because they are perfectly contented to be alone, intellectually speaking, with their minds. Mr. and Mrs. College Graduate, though their mental resources are supposed to be infinitely greater, will be, if alone, reading; otherwise, talking or playing bridge—anything *but* alone with their minds. Mr. and Mrs. Potterer, cast on a desert island, would equal the output of Robinson Crusoe and the Swiss Family Robinson at their collective best: Mr. and Mrs. Reader would die of ennui within a period of weeks.

Now if one grants all this—and I think one really must—one must also grant that the housewife of intellectual habits is in dire need of entertainment during her working day. Conversation is a dead loss. The fresh-vegetable man and the remover of the garbage pail can be detained only so long, your baby and their invalid wives being subjects of infinite exhaustibility. Little chats with the children, who if they are in the house at all are presumably under school age, are trying at their best.

"Mummy, is the moon rilly made of green cheese?"

"No, dear, of course not."

"What is it made of then, Mummy?"

"Why—er—of some sort of rock, dear."

"Of a *big* rock, Mummy?"

"Yes, dear."

"Of a big, *big* rock, Mummy?"

"Yes, dear."

"Of a big, *big*, BIG rock, Mummy?"

"Yes, dear."

"Of a ———"

And so on.

Anybody who has tried the combination of reading and housework can catalogue the pages of her book according to various domestic accidents. Page 42: finger cut while peeling peaches. Page 99: hole burned in shirt while ironing. Page 312: dish dropped while wiping. The lower right-hand corner of every page in every book in her library is also marked with sudsy water, dust, or beet juice.

Our entertainment, then, is obviously limited to the radio, on which, ideally, we are able to make the choice of four types of program: soap opera—to which we are too intellectual to listen; news; "hints" programs—fashion, cookery, gardening, and so forth; and music, "good" and otherwise.

The news and the hints programs are quickly disposed of. The first are not numerous enough or long enough to engage one's attention for over a few minutes at a time—and, of course, they are necessarily self-limiting. News commentators—who, like quiz programs, are wrong enough of the time to give you a pleasant feeling of superiority—save their efforts for the evening hours, when the brains of the family come home. The hints programs face much the same list of objections except that extreme limitedness of appeal and a certain adenoidal quality in their conductors must be added. Gardening hints are useful only to those who 1) are interested in gardening, 2) have time to garden, and 3) have a garden. Cooking hints are utterly without value if you cannot write down the recipes—which, of course, you cannot at the time of day at which cooking hints are offered. Fashion hints are the worst. They bring on dark broodings as to the probable effect of spattering pork chops on that old black velvet remade into a "sweet little house dress"—and thus only add to our sad state.

Music, "good" and otherwise—or perhaps I should say "music" and music—is certainly of wide appeal. But popular songs, which are the most readily available on the radio, consist, over a 14-hour stretch, of perhaps thirty songs played five times each and five songs played thirty times each. Let us admit without further discussion that along strictly hedonistic principles that kind of radio listening does not pay. But "good" or classical music is another matter. Such listening improves the mind, soothes the nerves and, needless to say, adds to one's knowledge of music. There is only one trouble: over a 14-hour period, one can hear classical music, certainly; one cannot *listen* to it.

I submit in all humility that in musical knowledge I am probably the most completely average woman in the world. I mean by this that my record is 100 per cent success in telling the *Bolero* from Brahms' *Lullaby*; 100 per cent failure in distinguishing between late Bach and early Mozart. On the basis of this combined boast and confession, I claim that no person of average musical knowledge can concentrate his whole mind on music for any length of time exceeding an hour or two at most. Any musical amateur who maintains seriously that he can listen to an entire symphony concert or opera without experiencing slight wanderings of the eye and mind I should hesitate to trust with my silver. Music simply does not and cannot hold our attention for long enough periods to count as entertainment for our 14-hour day, and we must therefore, along with those other offerings of radio which we have discussed, disqualify it for our purposes.

What happens now to the housewife's mind as she washes the dishes, listening to news, hints, and music? Horror of horrors, it is once more cast back upon its own resources!

My resources, during those hours of the automatic and unvarying labor of the woman who does not "work," consisted of much self-pity and much bitter cogitation on the sad lot of woman. My conclusions I related in unrelenting detail every evening to my patient and sympathetic husband, who was only very occasionally driven to point out that my only alternative was to leave the baby on a handy doorstep and make the acquaintance of a wealthy gentleman with a view to eventual elopement.

But one day my husband came home to find a pleasant wife, all sunshine and sweetness and gratitude for her happy lot. I had made the choice between snobbery and sanity. I had dis- covered soap opera!

More learned articles have probably been written about the evolution of the story than about the atomic bomb, and quite rightly, for the story forms an incredibly large part of our daily lives. All conversation, and all writing, is in story form or illustrated by stories. The chatter at dinner between Mummy, Daddy, and Junior usually takes the form of:

"Wait till I tell you what I heard about Mary Parker . . ."

"A man who came into the office today had had an interesting experience . . ."

"The *funniest* thing happened in arithmetic today . . ."

One of the most frequent demands of the bored child is "Mummy, tell me a story." What is more natural, then, than for the bored woman to make the same demand of her radio? And radio, with all the resources in its power, answers, "Yes, dear."

Of radio stories, commonly called soap opera, there is an infinite variety; and what is far more important, there are in- finite numbers. Every 15 minutes, from ten in the morning till six at night, there is another and more engrossing tale on the air. For 12 of every 15 minutes we can suffer with Mary Noble, sympathize with Joyce Jordan, hate Carson McVickers with a cold and deadly hatred. Only during the commercials—or for approximately three minutes of every quarter hour—can we brood about our unhappy fate. For soap operas, whatever their effect on the more critical faculties of our minds, *do* engross us. They *do* entertain us. They *do* keep our minds unwaveringly fixed on whatever program our radio is tuned to, and we enjoy them in the same open, wholesome and uncritical way that we enjoy a Perry Mason mystery, a Bob Hope movie, or Terry and the Pirates.

This quality, after all, is our only criterion. All we want from radio is continuous entertainment, something to fill our minds for 14 hours a day. And the combination of our mental requirements and our mental limitations makes this not alone the best, but the only, kind of program adequately to fill the bill.

If a fully trained staff—nurse, cook, and housemaid—were to turn up on my doorstep tomorrow morning with words to the effect that their dearest wish was to work for me, free, 11:30 A.M. might find me reading or playing golf. As it is, no power on earth, at 11:30 A.M. will keep me from discovering what Anna did after Barry threw away his chance for promotion in a fit of pique because she was late for dinner. Under different circumstances 1:30 P.M. might find me finishing a leisurely lunch with a friend. As things are, I can hardly wait to see if Lord Henry will be influenced by the caddish insinuations everybody seems to be making about his wife Sunday's character.

The upper intellectual brackets of housewifery, or the "readers," need, as we have seen, not less but more outside entertainment than those of lesser scholastic pretensions. It is, therefore, unfortunate that the soap opera is directed more to the latter, the "potterers," than to the "readers," for the readers need it far, far more. The solution to this, however, is not less soap opera, but better. I could wish, for instance, that our stories were not quite so much centered upon the home, of which we have what we ladies call "a tummy full." Portia is a lawyer, Joyce is a doctor, Mary Noble is at least a "backstage" wife, yet rarely do we learn anything of the legal, medical, and dramatic sides of their lives. I should like, also, to hear more complete stories during the daytime hours, but I realize that this would put on radio writers a burden more than the human mind could bear. The writer who was forced in sheer desperation to keep his characters in an elevator for an entire week, engaged in chit-chat, while he caught up with his story has my deepest sympathy. But our homey serials, after all, are only a little more monotonous than *Northanger Abbey*, only a little more complicated than *Of Time and the River*, only a little more silly than the collected silliness of a year's subscription to the *New Yorker*. And what woman would not trade a reading of these three works for the equivalent number of hours of mental emptiness?

Three things I find indefensible in radio; three things which, if remedied, would not detract in any way from its entertainment value. I cannot feel that it is necessary for radio children to say "ain't" in order to be childlike, or for young men to speak in Brooklyn or in South Chicago accents in order to prove their virility, or for old people to sprinkle home truths quite so freely in their conversation. To be told, as I was by Ma Perkins this afternoon, that "the more glamorous the people, the less stable" may be balm to my housebound soul, but it is totally untrue.

Annoying as these small mannerisms are; degrading as it is to find our main source of entertainment in a medium despised by our betters, all this is as a pinprick compared with the glorious feeling of emerging with a sigh from "The Road of Life" to find that, once again, the dishes are done.

CHAPTER 14

Baby in the Bathroom

[A short story]

U*rged by Mr. Kahler to write more often, Aloïse Heath, now living in St. Petersburg, Florida, after the war, turned her hand to fiction, recounting in short-story form what happened the day two-year-old Jimmy locked himself in the bathroom. This would be the last piece ABH would actually send Mr. Kahler, despite repeated letters and phone calls. She was, as always, just about to get to it, but didn't. "Baby in the Bathroom" was published in* Ladies' Home Journal *in 1947.*

"Jimmy, Jimmy dear. Come out of the bathroom."

"No, sank you."

"Please, dear. Come on out."

"No, sank you."

"Jimmy, come out of that bathroom *at once!* Do you hear me?"

"You hear me?" said Jimmy. "You hear me? You hear me?"

"You don't want to be a bad boy, do you? Open the door, darling."

"Jimmy bad-boy. Oh, *bad*-boy!" (giggling.)

"Honey, don't you want some candy?"

"Want candy, mawther."

"Well, then, open the door and come and get it."

(Pause) "Mawther,—Jimmy want candy."

"Then open the door, dear."

(Another pause) "Mawther—*You* open door."

"Now listen to me, Jimmy. You locked the door. *You* can open it."

There was a barrage of kicks and blows on the bathroom door.

"Bad-boy mawther! I want candy. Open the door. Bad-boy mawther!"

Why, that's wonderful, his mother thought. That's really remarkable. Three sentences in a row, all connected by a sequence of thought.

"Jimmy, you're a bad boy and mother is going away." Mrs. Heath then walked downstairs and over to the next-door neighbor's.

"Bad-boy mawther, *bad*-boy mawther, BAD-boy mawther," came floating across the lawn after her.

Mrs. O'Hara is a small, very neat, very precise person, and since the Heaths had moved into the house next to hers only 48 hours before, Mrs. Heath was a little dubious as to the impression as a brand-new neighbor she was making.

"You see, Mrs. O'Hara, he's only just two. I know he *can* open the door, but he's not himself, exactly. The excitement of coming to a new place, and he's—he's only *just* two," she trailed off desperately.

Mrs. O'Hara smiled warmly, "I'll talk to him, dear."

And Mrs. O'Hara led the way across the lawn and into the house.

Jimmy was once more in his "BAD-boy mawther" routine.

"Jimmy," said Mrs. O'Hara. "Jimmy dear, open the door."

"No, sank you," said Jimmy.

"Jimmy, come out of that bathroom at *once*, do you hear me?"

"You hear me?" said Jimmy. "You hare me? You hoor me?"

Mrs. O'Hara bent suddenly over the door knob. "There's a keyhole in this knob, dear. You haven't any keys around, have you?"

"Just trunk keys, and even those seem to be sort of misplaced."

Mrs. O'Hara went into the bedroom and called out of the window, "Betty, oh, Betty!"

A pretty dark head popped out of one of Mrs. O'Hara's windows.

"Betty, just run over here with our keys, will you, dear?"

"*All* the keys, Mother?"

"*All* the keys, dear" (firmly). "This is an emergency."

While Mrs. O'Hara tried the keys, Betty tried to make Jimmy open the door. Besides candy, she gave Jimmy the impression that awaiting him were apples, lollipops, ponies, and rides on the choo-choo. Jimmy didn't open the door, but he didn't call Betty a bad boy either. Betty has quite a way with children.

"Betty, run over and ask Mr. Jenkins to get the ladder. He's home this morning." And Mrs. O'Hara started on the 36th key.

Mr. and Mrs. Jenkins, looking like crime and punishment, came back up the stairs with Betty.

"Vinnie," said Mr. Jenkins—he was the one who looked like Crime—"sometimes I wonder about you. Would I be home if it weren't for my lumbago? And would I try to pry that ladder down with this lumbago?"

"Why, that's too bad, Fred dear. That really is too bad."

"You can't tell *me* that all you women can't get a two-year-old out of that bathroom because he won't open the door!"

"Now, Fred," Mrs. Jenkins said soothingly.

"Now, Fred," said Jimmy. "Now Fred. Now Frid. Now Frood."

Mr. Jenkins stood looking at Mrs. Heath. He was slightly wall-eyed, and she kept wishing he either wouldn't or wasn't.

"Is he afraid of his father?" he finally asked.

"Well, not so very," said Mrs. Heath humbly.

Mr. Jenkins jiggled the door knob. "Baby," he cooed in a strange sugary voice. "This is daddy, dear. Open the door."

"No, sank you," said Jimmy.

"Baby," bellowed Mr. Jenkins, "open that door, or daddy'll whale the living daylight out of you."

There immediately followed a rain of kicks and a tornado of shrieks. Jimmy could easily out-bellow Mr. Jenkins.

"Bad-boy man. Go way. Jimmy not like. Jimmy spit. Bad-boy man!"

Spit! Another new word, Mrs. Heath thought. And just two!

Mr. Jenkins' face was getting alarmingly red.

A ringing call from the O'Hara's lawn saved Mr. Jenkins' sanity.

"Hey, Mom! Hey, Mom! I'm home. Where are you?"

The five of them moved to the bedroom window.

Two boys of Henry Aldrich age stood outside gazing up at them.

"Michael O'Hara, what are you doing home from school at this hour?"

"Teachers' meeting, Mom. Joe came too."

"I noticed! Peanut-butter sandwiches and all the milk you want. That cold chicken in the icebox *is for tonight*."

"Mrs. O'Hara," Mrs. Heath broke in, "we've got some men now. Or practically. I mean, they're strong."

"*I'm* a man," bellowed Mr. Jenkins.

"Oh, I'm *sure* you are, Mr. Jenkins. I meant—well, you know, men without lumbago. I mean—well, *you* know, a man with lumbago . . ."

Mrs. O'Hara saved her. "You're quite right, dear." (Turns back to the window and calls) "Michael! You boys get the ladder and set it up beneath the bathroom window. We'll meet you outside."

The boys finally got the ladder placed to Michael's satisfaction and Joe climbed up.

An excited little pink face appeared at the window and two little fists pounded at the screen.

"Looka me, mawther," called Jimmy. "Looka me."

She looked around to see if everyone noticed how extraordinarily handsome her son was, but nobody seemed to.

"Hel-lo nice boy," said Jimmy.

So friendly, too. But nobody seemed to notice that either.

"Hey, kid, see that knob over there, on the door? Well, turn it."

"Tell him you'll give him candy, or something," said Betty.

"Tell him what you'll give him if he doesn't," shouted Mr. Jenkins.

Words began to gush forth from Joe. "Hey, kid, want some candy? Want some Coke? Well, turn that little knob over there."

"Want candy," Jimmy howled. "Want Coke. Open door, bad-boy."

Joe turned toward them a face that was beginning to look old beyond his years. "He won't," he said, in a small voice.

"Won't, *won't!*" scoffed Mr. Jenkins. "I'd like to hear any two-year-old tell *me* he won't . . ."

"One just did, dear," said Mrs. O'Hara mildly. "If the child won't, he won't. We'll just have to think of something else."

Mrs. Heath moved closer. "Joe" (she spoke in a subdued voice), "Joe, how does he look? Does he look all right?"

Joe peered through the opening in the window. "*He* looks all right—except—did he have any clothes on when he went in?"

"Well, naturally! He had on the sweetest little yellow rompers . . ."

"Not now," Joe broke in. "Not a stitch."

"No! Really, Joe? Shoes too? Just think of that! And all by himself! He's only JUST two, you know."

"I know," said Joe. "Do you want to hear how the bathroom looks?"

"Oh, Joe! Not—not the shaving cream?"

"Yes'm." (Glumly) "And bath salts in the bathtub. And talcum powder on the mirror. And water on the floor. Right now he's at the toothpaste—Mrs. Heath, I could make holes in the screen where the catches are and push it in."

"That's right," bawled Michael. "Smash up a fifty-dollar screen. Go ahead."

"Michael O'Hara," said Mrs. O'Hara, "sometimes I wonder how you ever got into a lovely family like mine. Joe, open those windows as wide as you can and push the screen in."

The window open, Joe wriggled through. Mrs. O'Hara waited. A little later Jimmy, naked as a jay bird, tore out of the house and hurled himself into his mother's arms.

"Oh, Jimmy. You're really a bad boy, darling."

"Jimmy bad-boy," said Jimmy, shaking his head mournfully. He looked around the group, fixed his eyes on Mr. Jenkins, and giggled. "Jimmy bad-boy," he informed him with pride. "Oh, bad-boy!" A bird alighted on the lawn, near the corner of the house, and he struggled out of his mother's arms and after it. "Jimmy catchum bird. Looka me. Jimmy catchum bird." He disappeared.

Mrs. Heath rose hastily. The atmosphere felt almost cool. "Well" (uncertainly), "I really can't thank you all enough. I don't know what . . ."

A babel of voices broke in.

"Before I'd let a child of *mine* . . ." said Mr. Jenkins.

"A little tap or two," said Mrs. Jenkins.

"Good scolding, at least," said Betty.

"When *I* was a kid . . ." said Michael and Joe in unison.

Mrs. O'Hara smiled reassuringly at Mrs. Heath, shrugged her shoulders, raised her eyes skyward—and froze. One by one, the little group faltered into silence as they turned their eyes in the direction of Mrs. O'Hara's increasingly glassy stare.

Jimmy's face appeared at the bathroom window. "Looka me, mawther," he called. "Jimmy shut door. Jimmy bad-boy, oh, *bad*-boy!" Jimmy giggled.

Just a regular boy, that's what he is, his mother thought. But she didn't say anything.

CHAPTER 15

Horizontal-Enrichment:
Information-Wise

Christmas 1965 caught ABH by surprise. The article she had planned to write for the Christmas issue of National Review she had not even started four days before the deadline. In desperation she rushed to a bookstore, took one incredulous look at the lavish array of books proffered for Christmas giving, and concluded: Give them to anyone in the world you like—or better still, don't like—but not to me. She gets in, en passant, a few licks at one of her, and James Thurber's, favorite subjects: The War between the Sexes.

Horizontal-enrichment, as I'm sure you already know, it's just that I can't take a chance on it, is knowing a little something about almost everything. Vertical-enrichment, naturally, is knowing practically everything about very little. Vertical-enrichment right now is In, I don't know why. Horizontal-enrichment is Out. Nobody wants to be broadly educated; they want to be intensively educated: a foolishness which I attribute to the Sputnik and those other scientific things. Dr. Spock, for instance, is an example of a vertical education topped off with vertical-enrichment. He knows so much about babies that he has even realized they can grow up without the benefit of as much knowledge as Dr. Spock can offer them; and I personally believe that he has taught so many generations of young mothers to relax and leave their children to Topsy's method that he has no more patients. This is not to be confused, however, with horizontal-enrichment. This is horizontal impoverishment: in fact, the nearer Dr. Spock gets to the oriental horizon the closer he comes to the educational level of the U.S. poverty program.

To be sure this is not wholly Dr. Spock's fault. There is such a thing as being so very very vertically enriched that the last time someone disagreed with you is lost in the mists of the past and you would lose it too if you were Dr. Spock or even Bertrand Russell.

Still: sometime, somewhere, someone must have given Dr. Spock a book for Christmas. It's the kind of thing one does give the children's pediatrician, cognac being as high as it is. And certainly no parents would exhibit such an appalling lack of tact as to present Dr. Spock with a book calculated to vertically enrich him. One just does not give a baby doctor a book on the Care and Feeding of Babies.

So what do you give for Christmas, unless you're of the "ties for the gentlemen, handkerchiefs for the ladies" school? You give books, horizontally enriching books. For one thing, if you're very careful, you can read them first. In the event, though, that you haven't begun your own book-browsing this year I really do think I'd skip it. What you would read is too expensive; and what you can afford is too cheap.

In the field of general knowledge, which is a field from which I like to make my purchases because I love being horizontally enriched even if it is Out, which would you want me to give you, for instance, *Russian Philosophy* in three volumes? One thousand, two hundred and sixty-seven pages? Twenty-two fifty? Well, you can't have it. Yes, frankly, I'd rather have $22.50 than your thanks.

How about *Textiles of Ancient Peru and Their Technique,*

also $22.50. You can't have that either. If the technique of Peruvian textiles is as sloppy as their grammar I wouldn't buy it for $2.50. Or them. How about *Sex and the Adult Woman* or *Football and the Single Man* (which incidentally, I know a man who is going to have football *and* the single life, or just me)? How about the most general piece of information I've ever seen on the cover of a book, *Wall Paintings by Snake Charmers of Tanganyika*, or Erle Stanley Gardner's *Hunting Lost Mines by Helicopter*, or *The Burned-Over District: The Social and Intellectual History of Enthusiastic Religion in Western New York, 1800–1850*?

Another book that I would very much like to give in order to read it is *The Prose of Ossip Mandelstam*, "a member of the Acmeist School of poetry whose master was Innokenti Annensky"—you know, the Annensky who taught Greek at the famous Lycée in Tsarkoe Selo! but I won't because I think he's a joke: Even the *Saturday Review* may have its waggish moments. There's a book on the history of the Self-Winding Watch whose jacket proclaims that it "contains an unusual *amount* of rare illustrations." And it had better if that sentence is an example of its prose. Then there's the *Encyclopedia of U.S. Government Benefits* crammed into 1,011 pages. Seven ninety-five, and a bargain I say. *Galaxies, Nuclei and Quasars* I will not give you because it wouldn't interest me. Nor will I give you *The MacArthur Controversy and American Foreign Policy* by Schlesinger and Rovere because I already know what it says. As for *What's in Mommy's Pocket-book?*, what on earth is the author thinking of? Johnny knows what's in Mommy's pocket-book. That's where he spends his spare time.

An animal book is pretty safe for almost everyone and the one I hope I get is either *The Personality of the Bird* or *Genetics and the Social Behavior of the Dog*. That musical transcription of macaw mating-calls I really don't think I could ever do anything with. Nobody will give me what some lucky person will certainly get, *Does Polly Want a Cracker?: Teach Your Bird to Speak Carefully.*

The Secret of Cooking for Cats has, I imagine, been well kept heretofore but is now being divulged by Martin A. Gardner because, he explained, "cats are complex characters. They have whims. They have prejudices. They have sensitivity. And making their meals interesting will provide many happy hours for all of you." The book features soups, fish, meat, and vegetable dishes, and a tasty selection of recipes which supply roughage. One which I can personally vouch for is called "Mew-Mew Gai-Pen." The recipe calls for "a small amount of boned fish, two oz. of cooked instant rice, three teaspoons of seasoned tomato juice, and just a dash of garlic powder. Place fish in bowl. Add instant rice. Mix well. Top with juice. Sprinkle with powder. Warm well. Serve." (Well, it sounds better than "*Oreille et pied de porc avec haricot rouge,*" which appears in that classic example of a self-contradictorily titled book: *The Art of Simple French Cookery.*)

Not even Polly's diction, when she asks for a cracker, is as fascinating as the sex life of animals, which is, in fact, the title of a foot-stool-sized book by Herbert Wendt, who "presents his always absorbing story with humor, directness, and complete objectivity," says the jacket. Quite correctly in my opinion, though I did think that the author showed a we-e-e-e bit of partiality to the paramecium. Plate #VII, "Paramecia in conjugation" just isn't all that interesting, let alone illustrative, and I suspect Dr. Wendt devoted nine drawings to them just to get them a little extra attention, and why shouldn't he to be sure? Dr. Wendt is full of surprises. Roman snails, for instance, are sadists. Did you know that? The reproduction of the nautilus is *not* completely understood as you and I had always believed, for the matter of the freely swimming hectocotylus arm has *never been solved!*

One warning. If you should ever own the book keep it out of the hands of children. Chapter IV, Section 8, "The Love

Factory of the Termite" is far too raw for the pre-adolescent: and small children will perhaps be disillusioned (and aren't we all?) when they learn that the gallant drake pursuing his abducted mate and her ravisher does not have rescue in mind but only the location of her approaching dishonor so he can pick her up afterwards and chase her back to sit on the babies.

I won't spoil your fun, but there is many a hearty chuckle to be found in Chapter VII: "Aberrations of the Libido in Mammals."

A hearty chuckle is really what you want at Christmas time, anyway, don't you? There is enough of that on the book shelves to last you the rest of the year. Here's *God Bless Everybody*, shades of Charles Dickens! By Mr. Average Citizen. Oh, well, maybe not that one. It says here: "A hard-hitting exposé of the un-Christian thinking and acting of so-called Christians that prevent America from fulfilling her grand destiny. 'EXPLO-SIVE,' 'CONTROVERSIAL,' 'EVERYBODY SHOULD READ IT.' (Information on page 132 could save your job. Information on page seven could save your life. Send $1 to . . .)" This one is better: *The Happy Child at the Piano*—not that I've ever seen one. *French Is Fun!* Well, I think that's a little positive, don't you? *Fun with Crewel Embroidery*. No. *Favorite Operas to Read and Hum*. No. *Polyominoes: The Fascinating New Recreation in Mathematics* by Solomon W. Golomb. A polyomino, it appears, is what a domino is two of and a trimono is three of and a pentamino is five of, which *you* never knew before, Buster. (Puzzles range widely in difficulty; one construction had 2,339 solutions.) The compendium contained almost one hundred problems including "absorbing games with polyominoes of more than two dimensions offering the reader weeks of diversion, for once you begin to make pentamino patterns you will find you cannot stop."

Did you notice the word "game"? "absorbing"? "diversion"? Every one of them is a cunning, conscious, calculated, *black* LIE. Polyominoes are nothing in the world but Geometry, and worse. There are 135 pages of theorems (". . . considering two or more dimensions, Gordon had exhibited a quasi-polyomino of 3-D cells—where D is the dimension—that cannot be used to cover or 'tile' the space. Actually this family of examples turns out to be one of *pseudo-polyominoes*") to be learned and exercises to be done before you are even offered any one of the "diversions." Ah! Not that the author calls his little nifties diversions once he's got you past the jacket! In the body of the book he really tips his hand. All those diversions are now problems, and this time, he isn't lying.

That book, *that* book is the one I bought for myself. In broad daylight, in full possession of my senses, I bought that book for $6.12 including tax when I could have bought seven Gothick paperback suspense-laden romances reminiscent of Daphne du Maurier's *Rebecca* for the same price—oh fool, *fool!*

Now that I've told you everything about the books not to give people, and I promise I won't give them to you either, okay?, the year 1965 has seen a magnificent contribution to the sum of human knowledge and its discoverer, along with so many of the great ones of the earth, will undoubtedly not be fully recognized until she is long dead. Not to go into detail, which would indeed be impossible let alone an injustice to the subject. But may I assure you that *The Avocado Pit Growers' Indoor How-To Book* by Hazel Perper will fulfill all your expectations no matter how high. You have a surprise waiting for you in the question so long considered to be definitively settled, of the number of toothpicks used to suspend your pit. I will not spoil it for you. And, wait till you read the astounding discovery about the water temperature; till you absorb detailed descriptions of the small but oh so significant differences between this avocado pit and that avocado pit.

I shall not go on, but oh my friends and oh my foes if Santa Claus should tuck Miss Perper's masterpiece into your stocking this year it will be a happy Christmas for you indeed.

CHAPTER 16

Before You Say No . . .

O*ne of her children's playmates, a boy who lived next door, asked Mrs. Heath to write him a recommendation for a Catholic prep school he was hoping to attend. Mrs. Heath obliged. The boy's letter and subsequent exchanges—with the boy, his brother, and the headmaster of the school—originally published in Na-tional Review in 1958, were picked up and republished by* The Reader's Digest.

March 7, 1958

Dear Mrs. Heath:

I wish to ask you a great favor. My brother David goes to Cranwell and he says they go easier on brothers, so I might have a chance to get in even though my grades aren't so terribly good. But I need three letters of recommendation and I have one from a priest and one from a nun and my father says he thinks the third one better be from someone who is not a priest or a nun. You are not a priest or a nun but yet you know me intamitely from me having delivered your paper even that bad day right after Christmas when their was no school and the *Times* boy didn't deliver his customers, and from those Catholic Christmas cards you always buy, and from the jack lantern pumpkins I helped you carve three years in a row, and the Easter Eggs, and a lot of other things. (Like the time I picked up John when he broke his arm and taught Priscilla how to ride a two-wheeler.)

Before you say no, I did break the trampoline but I didn't honestly know how heavy I was, because I grew very suddenly and the only reason I was always on the roof was because of my gliders which you said I could get if they were on the roof, and the time you wouldn't let me come in your back yard for three weeks that time, Word of Honor, John started it and it was not my fault because Scout's Honor, I only gave John the most compleatly gentle kind of tap so he would go home so Georgie Cunningham wouldn't beat him up, because you know how Georgie is when he gets mad. Because John threw a mud ball at him on his bicycle. Not that you were wrong, but that I'm explaining now, because you were so mad that you wouldn't give me a chance to explane, because John got their first and he fed you a lot of garbage. But I still like John, he is a fine young boy, he has been well brought up by his Mother.

But even if sometimes you don't get along with me too well, I always think of you as my "Oldest Friend" so I hope you will do me this great favor of writing me a letter of recommendation.

Thanking you for your trouble,

Respectfully yours,
PETER BAILEY-GATES

P.S. Thank you for the pennies of which I already had the 1926 San Francisco mint but I did not have the 1921 Denver. Do you have a 1905 Indian Head, I will pay one nickel, clear profit of four (4) ¢?

Respectfully yours,
PETER BAILEY-GATES

Dear Peter:

I would be glad to write you a letter of recommendation to Cranwell, and I am very flattered that you asked me. Of course,

I will have to tell the Truth, the Whole Truth, and Nothing But the Truth, so I hope nobody will be careless enough to allow my letter to fall into the hands of the police. I can't tell you how much I would miss you if you had to spend the next ten years in a reformatory.

Respectably yours,
MRS. H.

P.S. No, I haven't got a 1905 Indian Head, which saddens me very much, but what saddens me more is that even after three years' acquaintanceship you don't know me well enough to realize that I also know that this particular penny is worth $6.00! You and your 4¢ profit—hah! I've told you and told you about my high I.Q. Don't you believe me? However, just to show you I bear no grudge, I will give you my duplicate of the 1911 no mint mark—for free yet!

Respectably yours,
MRS. H.

P.P.S. Don't worry about my letter. I will bet you one dollar (from me) to one doughnut (from you) that you will get into Cranwell—not because you're such a hot-shot, you understand, but because if I'm crazy enough to like you, your priest and your nun are probably suffering from the same form of insanity. On the other hand, they may know you even better than I do, God help them!

Respectably yours,
MRS. H.

March 9, 1958

To Whom It May Concern:

Peter Bailey-Gates has been in and out of my house almost daily for the past three years—by "almost" I mean those short sentences of exile which I have been unkind enough to impose upon Peter—and in that time I have come to know him very well indeed: as friend, paper boy, fellow penny-collector, and as combined decorator, waiter, and entertainer at my younger children's birthday parties.

I have found Peter to be unfailingly good-humored, well-mannered, and considerate—all of which qualities stand him in good stead in his relations with the public, which are many and varied. I am sure that no boy in New England, much less in West Hartford, has been engaged in so many intricate business enterprises as Peter Bailey-Gates. I have bought, hired, subscribed to, invested in, paid and been paid interest on fully a dozen of his ventures in the last three years—not even counting his snow-shoveling, leaf-raking, apple-picking, and garbage-can-toting, for which my own young sons are recruited. Peter's financial sense is, however, no deterrent to his feeling for what is fitting and proper: when he washed the car of the seventy-year-old spinster who lives nearby, for instance, he was careful to explain (lest I should find out, I suppose) that he had refused payment only because she had "no man to make money for her"; again, when he asked me to take an ad in his projected Colony Road News and I was so irreverent as to reserve two inches of space for the slogan "Hooray for Mrs. Heath," Peter offered to refund my dollar because he had caused my ad to appear as "Compliments of a friend" instead. I must, however, state categorically that Peter has faithfully and conscientiously fulfilled his share of every and any contract between us, whatever it may have been. (And the fact that one or two of these contracts have been rather clearer to Peter than to me, has been indignantly attributed by my own children to my habit of doing jigsaw puzzles, reading, watching television programs, and saying, "Uh-hunh" simultaneously, when I should have been listening. My husband affirms this judgment.)

Lest my young friend sound barely lower than the angels, I must add that his fertile imagination combined with his 13-year-old sense of humor have led, on occasion, to my addressing him with harsh words and unkind—("You know perfectly well that when I told you last Tuesday you could climb up on the roof to get your glider, I didn't mean you could buy ten more gliders and aim them at the—and by the way, I hope you didn't buy them with the lottery money for the bicycle horn—when are you going to have that lottery, anyway? I bought those tickets six weeks ago!" And much more.). These irrational, if predictable crises of the adult world leave Peter possibly repen-tant, probably remorseful, but certainly unruffled. He is more sophisticated today than three years ago, when, at the age of ten, he frequently urged me not to get my liver in a quiver. Today, when Peter and I have what he refers to as "a difference of opinion," he retires with complete equanimity to his own back yard until such time as my ill-humor subsides. My change of mood is apparently picked up by Peter's extrasensory percep-tion within the hour, for whenever I decide that the time has come for forgiving and forgetting, he appears at my front door within 15 minutes, to assure me *he* has forgiven and forgotten. By way of proof (or penance?) he then resumes without rancor his status as our daily visitor.

Needless to say, our friendship is steadfast.

ALOISE BUCKLEY HEATH
(*Mrs. Benjamin Wild Heath*)

March 15, 1958

Cranwell Preparatory School
Office of the Principal

Mrs. Benjamin Wild Heath
29 Colony Road
West Hartford, Connecticut

Dear Mrs. Heath:
I am very grateful to you for your detailed and colorful description of Peter Bailey-Gates.

Many of Peter's accomplishments can be put to good use at School. Leaf-raking and snow-shoveling are part of the punitive curriculum. Endowed with all the energy which you describe, I am sure that Peter will be an early candidate for demerits.

We will try to keep pace with Peter. What substitute we will have when the occasion arises for Peter to "retire to his own back yard" we will try to figure out during the year.

Sincerely yours,
CHARLES E. BURKE, S.J.
(Rev.) Charles E. Burke, S.J.
Principal

March 15, 1958

Dear Mimi and Dad:

Please excuse the paper, for I'm in study hall, and since something happened tonight, which made me feel pretty proud of my little (little? Ha Ha) brother Peter, I thought I'd tell you about it, unless you already know. This has also changed practically my entire attitude toward Father Burke who has practically never been known to crack a smile in the memory of the oldest graduate.

Not more than five minutes ago, during the break between study hall hours, Father Burke called me and showed me a letter which Mrs. Heath had written to him about Peter. It described Peter to a tee. All of the letter was praiseworthy about him, and had been written just about Peter and nothing else. Father Burke was astonished and asked me if it was all true, and I told him it was, and he said in that case Peter gets in!! . . .

Say hello to the little kids for me please, and tell them "Big Dave" will be home soon.

Love and prayers,
Your son DAVID

March 15, 1958

Dear Pete:

Boy, does Mrs. Heath sure have your number. Father Burke said he can hardly wait to get you up here to knock it out of you. Love and kisses.

DAVE

CHAPTER 17

Prosiness in Purple

Page 34 of the current issue of an immensely popular periodical devoted to furthering world knowledge and understanding of movie stars features the all-but-life-sized likeness of a rather pleasant-looking young man in a bathing suit. His name, the caption says, is Tab Hunter, and furthermore, the caption says: "Bet if we asked you . . . you could write a book—about the ways he talks, and whispers and . . . looks." (Punctuation theirs.)

National Review, one assumes happily, could not base a successful fund-raising drive on a bet of this kind. You, for one, certainly could *not* write a book about the way young what's-his-name talks, and whispers . . . and looks, could you? Well, it just happens, dear reader, that you are, as usual, in the minority. The readers of *Filmland, Hollywood Stars, Modern Screen, Movie Album, Movieland, Movie Mirror, Movie Show, Movie World, Photoplay, Screenland, Screen Parade, Screen Stars, Silver Screen*, etc., who outnumber you by many, many thousands, will take that bet and win it.

Between thirty and forty million Americans, it is claimed, are regular readers of one or more movie magazines, and, of these, several million read *ten or more a month. Every month!* The news dealer who is my informant tells me that when (and if) children outgrow comic books, they turn *en masse* to movie magazines. In late adolescence, the boys (ah! the questing male!)

abandon such immature literature for the real-true-crime, or the peek-and-pry kind of thing, but the girls, says my friend, never stop reading movie magazines at all—ever. Or they haven't in the thirty years my friend has been a news dealer.

Those who perused ten movie magazines this month, as did the unhappy Aloïse Heath, read six full-length articles about Pat Boone, five about Ava Gardner, five about Anthony Perkins, five about Natalie Wood, five about Jayne Mansfield, five about Tab Hunter (he's the one they bet you could write a book about the way he you-know-whats), and five about one Anthony Franciosa. (And don't say: "Who on earth are all these people?" *to me*, because I'm the girl who can tell you—this month anyway.)

Researchers into the literature of the silver screen have also read several hundred shorter features and several thousand "gossip" items, all of which say, as do the articles, exactly the same thing about exactly the same people. All of them have the drama, suspense, and just *sheer fun* of the following thriller (illustrated by four large photographs) which I quote in its entirety because it is even more like all the others than all the others are.

"Elvis Presley Double Date"

You have probably heard by now how Elvis Presley surprised Hollywood with his good manners and respect for the acting profession. Old-timers expected him to be a brash youngster with a know-it-all attitude, but he turned out to be quiet and hard-working. The two women in his latest film, *Loving You*, became very friendly with him while the movie was being shot so when the work was finished and they all had time for some socializing, one co-star, Liz Scott, invited Elvis to bring his other co-star, Dolores Hart, to her home for a casual afternoon at home. They toured Liz' handsome house on arrival, had lunch, sat in the garden and played cards and talked, talked, talked the whole time. In fact such a good time was had by all that the three agreed they would get together again very soon.

You think I made that one up, don't you? All right, *you* read *Movie Magazine*. Find out the hard way. The literature of the silver screen is, then, if you're still with me, stupefyingly dull, and it is objectively incredible that millions of people intelligent enough to read can notwithstanding read this kind of thing; unless of course they read them for the ads, for weird and wonderful things indeed are to be gleaned from the advertising columns of movie magazines. In fact after reading them you can only wonder why so few people are Absolutely Perfect. No gumption probably. The main advertising feature, as might be expected, is standard perfume-pomade-potion stuff, all guaranteed to contract or expand any desired area of the anatomy and to turn it the color, texture, and flavor that brings out the real *You*. (And that'll be the day: when thirty or forty million movie magazine readers have their real *Them* brought out. That'll be the day I move to Samarkand.)

The advertising columns also feature at least fifty, or what seems like fifty, books on the acquisition of charm, which in- volves a great deal more than you have hitherto believed. Be- sides telling you to be pretty, poised, punctual and to Find Out What His Interests Are, one book seems to devote an entire subsection to the fascinating problem of "How to Keep One Foot at Right Angles to the Other." (So help me.) Another book has an article on Smoking Prettily and still another what seems to be a complete chapter on "How to Lift One Eyebrow Alone Without Changing the Facial Expression." I think I'll send for that one, as a matter of fact; I've been wanting to raise one eyebrow lately.

(But first I intend to avail myself of the sensational, unparal- leled, for-a-limited-time-only, send only 75 cents plus 25 cents postage, offer of a ring bearing a 3-D image of Elvis Presley in full, glowing color. And the ad says his eyes seem to follow you everywhere.)

It is hardly surprising, of course, that readers of movie

magazines need charm and want Elvis Presley. What *is* surprising, to this lay-woman at any rate, is the fact that, according
to the advertising columns, at least 95 per cent of these readers
seem to suffer from the same exotic illness. For most of these
periodicals advertise no less than 15 different remedies for a
strange and horrible disease called psoriasis. I don't know what
psoriasis is, and I don't intend to look it up because it sounds
like the kind of thing I should like to continue to not know
about. It is obviously strange and horrible, however—otherwise
it would not be called psoriasis; it would be called chicken-pox,
or back-ache—and I feel that the fact that this malady is suffered
by a great majority of thirty or forty million Americans *all of
whom read movie magazines* is significant enough to demand
an immediate and intensive investigation by persons other than
myself, who am too busy.

Unfortunately, the non-commercial, or less directly commer-
cial columns of the movie magazines are far less interesting
than those paid for by the inch. From the literary, or, more
accurately, the literated standpoint, their language is not only
pretentious, but unforgivably incorrect: rumors are always *ripe*
in Hollywood, for instance; actors spend *torturous* years achiev-
ing success; Anthony Perkins "heatedly objects to being ag-
gressed"; Yul Brynner's favorite word is "Fahnstahstic!" The
prose is not so much purple as maroon; "But how many years
has he left in which to pander [sic, naturally] his one ace in
hole when it comes to stock-in-trade? . . . But he has simply
not suffered enough; he has not tasted the darker wine in life's
cup as yet, and as a result he lacks that tragic sense of life . . ."
etc.

Contrary to unpopular, or minority impression, however,
movie magazines are anything but sensational; their trash is of
the Disposall, not the septic-tank variety. Only her photographs
identify the Maureen O'Hara of *Photoplay* with the Maureen
O'Hara of *Confidential*, for movie stars, as us readers know

even if you don't, are Just Plain Folks Except Prettier. Nor do
the magazines allow any possible misinterpretation of the activities of the constellation members. When an actress tells us
that she and her husband simply "*dash* home to see our child—
we sometimes made it a race to see who can get there first,"
she quickly explains: ". . . but that's all in fun, of course. It
doesn't really matter." When Bette Davis says: "The best advice
ever given me was by Charles Laughton. He said, 'Never lack
the courage to hang yourself,'" she is careful to add: "Of course,
the term was used figuratively." (In other words Charles
Laughton did *not* recommend suicide, and Bette Davis did *not*
consider such a recommendation the best advice ever given
her. Because if he *had*, she *wouldn't*, but he *didn't*. See?)

Every article, item, or feature about a married actress currently living with her husband contains the words: "Small
wonder Mary spends her happiest hours in her favorite role—
Mrs. John Smith, housewife." Elizabeth Taylor's husband
informs a world which had rather suspected it that "Liz is
basically a woman." Nobody, but nobody, can be allowed to
deviate from Just Plain Folksiness: when Katharine Hepburn
tells a columnist that "if only men would pay more attention
to us homely girls, what affection they would get," the columnist adds hastily, "I've never thought of Katie as a homely girl,
have you? And she certainly had her share of affection and a
wonderful marriage in the early part of her career—it lasted
from 1928 to '35." (How wonderful, after all, can a marriage
get?) The other little clichés you already have at the tip of
your tongue. Like: "I have more fun just staying around the
house with my mother than I do going on dates," says Just
Plain Debra Paget; like: "Keep your thinking high and your
living simple," says Just Plain Terry Moore; like: "Whenever
I feel that I am growing too big for my britches, I ask myself,
'What will God think if I fail to live up to my responsibilities?'"
says Just Plain Pat Boone. (I couldn't actually *find* anyone who

said: "My philosophy is 'Open Up Your Heart and Let the Sunshine In,'" but someone did. Take my word for it.)

The normal person's craving for privacy is as pronounced in Hollywood as it is where you and I live, incidentally, and if you don't believe it, you can see, in each of two magazines this month, photographic sequences of a mother and daughter and of a husband and wife who have slipped away from photog- raphers to spend a day alone together. (Honest!) And, nervous Mothers' Circles to the contrary, the photographic staffs of movie magazines are just as concerned about Mothers' Circles as the editorial staffs—or vice versa. They feature many beauties in bathing suits, but very few girls in gauze; and in ten periodicals I came upon only one photograph which might give pause even to the movie-magazine-reading mother of a movie-magazine-reading daughter. This was a picture of Jayne Mansfield (40-18-35) at which four of *my* small daughters gazed in horror and apprehension. Did all grown-up ladies . . .? the eldest asked in hushed tones. Would even Pam and Priscilla and Alison and Betsey . . .? (No, I answered firmly, they would *not*. I, their mother, would see to it.)

The silver-screeners who are just simply not Plain Folks, no matter what your standards, are either More Sinned Against Than Sinning, or Crazy Mixed-Up Kids. Anthony Perkins, for instance, walked down Sunset Boulevard in his bare feet not because he was a nasty little show-off, but because "indiffer- ence, insecurity and non-conformity are apparently the spice of life these days." Elizabeth Taylor divorced her second hus- band because "a penalty of youth had encountered a penalty of middle-age. She still loved him. He still loved her." So there was nothing to do but part. Ingrid Bergman had a *terrible* time with Dr. Lindstrom: "Cold, dictatorial, unresponsive, he added a steam bath to their house and made no effort to enter his wife's world."

Marilyn Monroe has been suffering from a father complex

(you'd be amazed at how many of them have father complexes) which is now alleviated because "Arthur [Miller]'s refusal to name his former comrades [in the Communist Party] made Marilyn fully realize his tremendous courage and integrity." Ava Gardner married one man after another because she "rejects herself as a woman." All of the Crazy Mixed-Up Kids have redeeming features, however. Ava Gardner's is her courage. "'I have an affinity for jerks,' she once told a friend, 'but that won't stop me from looking for the right man! Every time I fall in love, or think I'm in love, I'll get married.'" As you can see, there speaks a good little girl, at heart. She said, get *married*, didn't she? *Que diable veux-tu encore?*

CHAPTER 18

A Trapp Family Christmas
with the Heaths

One of the reasons—I say one of the reasons because I could think of *several* others if I put my mind to it—that I kept on having babies for years after all my classmates were taking turns being president of the Planned Parenthood Association, was that I always thought a big family would be such fun at Christmas.

I even know why Ben Heath, who is tied to me by the bonds of marriage, has the Spirit of Christmas around Thanksgiving and the Spirit of Ash Wednesday around Christmas. I keep telling him I know. "I know," I say. "I know. I know. I know."

I know we always get more glitter and glue on the floor than on the candles and that I never remember to wipe it up until the dining-room carpet (new last January) is permanently (though not uninterestingly, I always think) spangled.

I know I look absolutely insane, crawling around in the snow for weeks before Christmas, putting candy canes on window sills and galloping madly off in the dark shouting "Ho! Ho! Ho! "

I know the newsboy would rather have two dollar bills than a $1.95 flashlight wrapped in green paper and silver ribbon, with "TO MERVYN" spelled out in red Scotch tape.

I know nobody can eat those Cut 'N' Bake cookies the children decorate as Christmas trees with green sugar and cinnamon hearts and then (too many cinnamon hearts) as Santa Claus with more cinnamon hearts and melted marshmallow and then (too much melted marshmallow) as angels with more melted marshmallow and pink crayon.

I know it's un-Gesell and not even altogether Spock to match candid blue eye to candid blue eye with a ten-year-old and say: "But, sweetie, how should *I* know why Polly's Santa Claus is really her father? Maybe her father *has* to be her Santa Claus, poor little thing! Maybe Santa Claus just doesn't *like* Polly. Did you ever think of that?"

I also know ten children, well, anyway, seven—who aren't going to read this.

I know all that. What I didn't know till this year was what Ben meant, every Christmastide, when he kept tossing out, not at all at random, the words "materialistic" and "spiritual." What I always thought he meant was that it would be materialistic for Alison and Betsey and Jennifer and Timothy to get a Chatty Kathy apiece, but spiritual for them to share one. I mean, that's what I thought until one afternoon last week.

That afternoon they were all in the coat closet (well, they *were*, that's all; they *like* the coat closet) making out their Christmas lists. Pam, who can spell, was helping the ones who can't write; and Alison, who is magic, was helping the ones who can't talk. I had my ear at the crack in the door, listening, because I'm still trying to hear one of those childhood conversations whose innocent candor tears at your heartstrings. You've read about them, I'm sure.

What I heard was my dear little ones calculating how much more each of them would get for Christmas if they didn't have so many brothers and sisters to share the loot. They itemized, giving reasons for their choice, the siblings they would gladly exchange for a hockey stick or an Army bugle or a Barbie doll with a different dress for every single day of the week. From what I could hear through the crack, *nobody* kept Buckley and Timothy, which is understandable—let's face it—but hardly nice.

Then and there I decided (yes, *again*) that there is more to old Ben than meets the eye and that this Christmas the Heaths would be spiritual. Spiritual *also*, I mean. At my age you just can't cut those old materialistic ways right out of your life like *that*. My resolve was easier than you think because, at the time, I happened to be reading a book called *Around the Year with the Trapp Family*. Actually, I was reading it to find out why the Trapps play the recorder better than we do, a fact which is widely bruited by those who have heard us, though not necessarily the Trapps. It turned out, though, that the Trapp family spends its year not practicing the recorder, as I had hoped, but in "Keeping the Feasts and Seasons of the Christian Year," which was, in fact, the subtitle of the book. We plunged into keeping the Christmas Season of the Christian Year like the Trapps. Some of us (me) plunged more enthusiastically than others (Jim, Pam, John, Priscilla, Buckley, Alison, Betsey, Jennifer, Timothy, Janet and their father).

Certainly, some of the things the Trapp family does at Christmas are not entirely suited to the Heath family. I know. I *know*. And some—give me that much—I didn't even try. Like baking the traditional *Speculatius* on December 6th (St. Nicholas' Day), for instance; or the traditional *Kletzenbrodt* on December 21st (St. Thomas' Day), or even the traditional *Lebzelten, Lebkuchen, Spanish Wind, Marzipan, Rum Balls, Nut Busserln, Cocoanut Busserln, Rum Stangerln, Pfeffernüsse*, and *Plain Cookies*, on December 23rd. Especially since the freezer was bulging with all those still Uncut'N'Unbaked rolls of cookie dough. Nor did I consider for more than one mad moment suggesting that everybody take a nap before Midnight Mass and that their father awaken them by initiating a procession from room to room with a lighted candle, singing "Shepherds

Up!" (each verse pitched a half-tone higher than the last), though I think it would be lovely, myself. Maybe when Ben is older ... mellower ...

We *did* make an Advent Wreath with four red candles, and it was beautiful; but John and Priscilla are Junior Fire Marshals, and though they said it was all right to hang the wreath from the ceiling on four red ribbons, they wouldn't even *discuss* letting us light the candles after it was hung. And, as a matter of fact, I know perfectly well that Ben Heath would light off for the South Seas before he would light the candles, stand under the wreath, read the Gospel for the Day and listen to the children sing: "Ye heavens, dew drop from above and rain ye clouds the Just One ..." Even if I could get the children to sing it. Are your children *giggly*?

The Trapps say that "Silent Night" should be sung for the first time on Christmas Eve, and they convinced me, and I convinced the children; which would have been enough to make me abandon the whole idea if I hadn't been so bemused with good will and all. It wasn't till I got the notes from Mr. Jones, Mrs. Miano, Mr. Segar, Mrs. Arnold, Miss Billinghan, Mrs. Brown, Mrs. Larratt and Miss Bates that I remembered that the Fourth Form Glee Club Concert, the Grade VII Carol Sing, the Grade VI Christmas Vespers, the Grade III Christmas Play, the Grade II Christmas Chapel, the Grade I Christmas Assembly, the Kindergarten Christmas Program and the Nursery School Christmas Party (to all of which I have been kindly invited) have three things in common: rehearsals, Heaths, and "Silent Night." *I quite understand*, I wrote Mr. Jones, Mrs. Miano, Mr. Segar, Mrs. Arnold, Miss Billinghan, Mrs. Brown, Mrs. Larratt and Miss Bates.

I really didn't see how the *Christkindl* custom could go wrong, though. I *still* don't. In the Trapp family, at the beginning of Advent, every one writes his name on a piece of paper and the papers are put in a basket which is passed around as

soon as the children have finished singing: "Ye heavens, dew
drop from above." Everybody picks a name from the basket,
and the pickee, if you follow me, becomes the picker's secret
Christkindl, and the idea is, you do your *Christkindl* a good
turn every day until Christmas without ever letting him know
who you are. It sounds simple, spiritual and also fun, doesn't
it? And it works out *beautifully* in the Trapp family. In fact,
from Advent until Christmas, the Trapp household resounds
with the glad cries of *Christkindlen* who have found their
shoes shined, their doll houses tidied up, and the table already
set the day it was their turn. But there *are* a few technical
problems that I feel you should know about, just in case you
plan to be spiritual next Christmas.

In our house, the first technical problem was Jim. Jim said
he was too old for this kind of thing, and I said, what did he
mean, too old; most of the Trapps are older than he is; and he
said, not those dumb kids that sang that dumb Do-Re-Mi song
aren't older than he is; and I said, well, if he thought he was
too old at 15, what did he think I was; and he said, too old at
42 (*never* tell children your age), but anyhow, I won because
after all, I'm the one who has to sign his Driver Education
Permission Slip—and also, if I didn't drive all over New England every Saturday to see the Kingswood J.V. wrestle, who
would? Then the others said, what about Timothy and Janet?
Timothy and Janet were too little to do good turns to their
Christkindlen, so why should they be anybody else's *Christkindl*? I said, I *must* say, this didn't sound very much like the
spirit of Christmas to *me*, and I would take care of the babies'
Christkindlen if everyone was so worried, and let's *draw*, for
Heaven's sake! So we drew, and five of them drew their own
names and Janet ate one, which turned out to be John, after
we hit her on the back. So we made another slip for John (a
piece of paper *our* baby has eaten is *distinctive*) and we drew
again and eight of them drew their own names. I said, maybe

it would work out better if I drew a name for each of them, and they said, No *sir*, not and have you know who everybody's *Christkindl* is and comparing what everybody did for their *Christkindl*, no *sir*, Mother, none of that stuff. Jim and Pam said that if they could have paper and pencil and peace and quiet they could probably work it out by mathematical prob- abilities, but it was getting pretty late, so I called them up by ages, and before Jim drew, I took out his name, and before Pam drew I took out her name and put back Jim's, and so on. (Well, unless I *tell* you, how will you ever know how to do it?)

When we had all drawn (which took far more time to do than to read about, no matter what you're thinking), everybody opened his little slip of paper "at a given signal." That's how the Trapps do it, and that's how we did it. I said; "Everybody ready? One. Two. Three. Open. Well, pick it up and open it *now*, Alison! Everybody does *not* have to fold their paper up again and forget the names they drew ... Besides, how could they? ... Not fold the papers, for Heaven's sake; forget the names! ... Well, all right ... All *right*, I said; we're *starting* over. Everybody ready? One. Really, Alison, anybody would think you were five and a half. Two. Three. Open. ALISON!!"

So we opened our little slips of paper at a given signal (the Trapps said "a" given signal, not which, after all) (what irritates me is that Alison can't even *read*!) and everybody learned the name of his secret—*secret*, mind you—*Christkindl*. This is another uniformly joyful moment in the Trapp family. At this moment in the Heath family, Jim looked up from his slip, glared at John and groaned. John looked up from his slip, glared at Jim and made vomiting noises. Priscilla said: "Oh, *Mother*, do I have to have that pest?" Buckley said: "Mother, how do you think that makes a poor little boy feel to have everybody in this whole absolute world call him a pest every absolute min- ute?" Everybody nudged everybody else. "Jim has John. John has Jim. Priscilla has Buckley," they told each other.

The non-readers came running up to find out who their *Christkindlen* were. "Pam," I whispered into Betsey's ear. "Pam," shrieked Betsey. "Betsey has Pam," everybody told everybody else. "Tim-Tim, but don't tell," I whispered into Jennifer's ear. She flung her arms around Timothy's head. "Tim-Tim, I *know* sumpeen. I *know* sumpeen, Tim-Tim," she roared. "Jennifer has Timothy," everybody told everybody else. The baby ate her paper again, but it was all right this time: I knew whose name she had eaten. I had arranged for us to draw each other, because we're in love.

A few minutes later they thundered upstairs to homework or bed, and even over the rattling of the window panes I heard the negotiations. "Well, then, will you trade Priscilla for Alison and a nickel? For Alison and a dime? For me not hiding your shell collection? For not hitting you in the stomach as hard as I can?"

Actually, it didn't turn out too badly. After a few days of such good turns as reporting that a *Christkindl* hadn't done his arithmetic because he was going to copy Georgie's before school tomorrow (and he just can't *learn* anything that way, *can* he, Mother?), or throwing a *Christkindl's* cherished leather jacket into the washing machine (because it was so absolutely *filthy* he could have got *germs* from it, Mother), or taking the batteries out of a *Christkindl's* flashlight because she reads under the covers after bedtime (and that's why practically *everybody* practically *constantly* goes blind, isn't it, Mother?), everybody was getting pretty tense. (Well, all right: bloody.) And in our family, when *everybody* is tense, *somebody* minds it enough to stop it. I don't know which of them found the solution to our *Christkindl* problem; all I know is every Sunday now, they each buy nine penny lollipops, and every night they slip a lollipop under their *Christkindl's* pillow. Well, I know that doesn't sound so terribly spiritual, but it's better than what they used to do. What they used to do was steal each other's lollipops.

I wouldn't want anybody to think that my baby and I have sunk to such a mundane relationship, though. We haven't had to change our routine at all. Every morning Janet allows her *Christkindl* to rock her a little, and every evening I rock my *Christkindl* a little.

CHAPTER 19

Merry Christmas to Everyone
in the World Except Men

That does sound a little harsh, doesn't it? Well, all right
then: MERRY CHRISTMAS to men, too, but under *no circumstances*
A HAPPY NEW YEAR. For one thing, if I said it, I wouldn't mean
it, which would be insincere and just like a woman, as we all
know: and for another thing, men don't need to be wished A
HAPPY NEW YEAR. How would you *keep* a man from having a
Happy New Year anyway? He may break his leg, of course, or
lose his wife, or go bankrupt, or land in jail, but 1963 can have
in store for him no vicissitudes that will shake his serenely
shining inner conviction that, all in all, he is just about perfect.

Every man is convinced that he is Trustworthy, Loyal, Helpful, Friendly, Courteous, Kind, Obedient, Cheerful, Thrifty,
Brave, Clean, Reverent; that he is intelligent, and that he has
beautiful eyes and an extraordinarily keen sense of humor. Like
all convictions, of course, some of these, sometimes, may be
shaken, but what cannot be shaken in man (you do realize that
when I say "man," I mean "men," don't you? When I mean
"people" I say "women") is the knowledge—the *knowledge*—
that whatever qualities he may or may not have, there is something he innately is: superior to women. In some black moment
a man may entertain the fleeting thought that he is not, after
all, so very Trustworthy, Loyal, Helpful, Friendly, Courteous,

179

Kind, Obedient, Cheerful, Thrifty, Brave, Clean, Reverent, or intelligent or pretty-eyed or humorous. He may realize, in fact, that he is a slob. But he is a *male* slob; you can't take that away from him (I wouldn't want to, myself) and the one thing a male slob is, is better than any woman, any time, any place. Not only do men "know" this, but so do their poor brainwashed wives, not to mention their parents, their sons, and those of their daughters who are not in their middle teens.

Oh, of *course*, there are men who don't *know* they are superior to women! There are hundreds of them, as a matter of fact, and they are all in mental institutions, finding out that they had bad mothers, which will cure them.

People started thinking along these lines, I suppose, shortly after it became apparent that whereas men generally ended up eating saber-toothed tigers, saber-toothed tigers generally ended up eating women; and that it took at least two women to help a man carry a dead pterodactyl home, because one woman alone kept dropping her end. But around the time the lever was invented—or, at the very least, the shotgun (well, *certainly* they were invented by men: who needed them?)—you would have thought that men could no longer feel superior to women without feeling, to the exact degree, inferior to levers, wouldn't you? Well, you would be wrong. A man is so constituted that he can spend an entire evening bragging about his horsepower without once considering where this puts the horse.

Now here, for the first time published ever, is the absolutely definitive list of the fields in which men excel women: athletics, arithmetic, musical composition, physical strength, singing baritone, and superiority.

Woman is, of course, a much better physical specimen. She operates more efficiently, under greater stress, with fewer breakdowns, on less fuel, for years longer than men. Men, on the other hand, at all ages eat like horses, die like flies, and suffer from constant malfunctioning of their relatively simple

apparati. They are also susceptible to exclusively male conditions like distichiasis, hypertrichosis, ichthyosis, and nystag-
mus, which are, respectively, double eyelashes, dense hairy
growth on the ears, barklike skin, and rhythmical oscillation
of the eyeballs. (Men who have all of these conditions at the
same time usually die without issue because no one will marry
them.) In between times, men don't feel very well. *But:*—the
average man can lift 75 pounds and the average woman can
lift 62 pounds; so that makes woman the weaker sex; what else?

The average man is well into his twenties before he is able
to get angry without trying to fight; and he is well into the
next world before he stops losing his temper, shouting, slamming doors, swearing. Twice as many men as women have
nervous breakdowns, three times as many commit suicide, four
times as many have ulcers, and there are fifty times more unpremeditated attacks and a hundred times more unpremeditated
murders by men than by women. But you know what women
do, don't you? Women *cry*! Women cry because women are
more emotional than men, that's why.

In all school intelligence tests given to students who are
receiving the same education, the boys, from preschool on up,
rate higher than girls in arithmetic. In every other testable
field, girls get better scores; and among boys and girls who have
identical aptitude scores, the girls do better in related achievement tests. So what does "everybody know"? Why, everybody
knows that mathematical ability is the *real* measure of intelligence! True, men have produced more geniuses than women,
but this isn't what men believe. Men don't go around saying:
"Albert Einstein is smarter than women"; they go around saying
"*men* are smarter than women"!

Everybody knows that there is only one really marvelous,
awesome, and completely satisfying achievement that a human
being is capable of, and that is to give birth to a baby; and
when small boys first realize that they can't and their sisters

can, they are quite understandably consumed with jealousy. All mothers know this and so do all very little boys, but nobody, apparently, has told the child psychologists. *Their* theory is that it is the little girls who become jealous when they realize they are different from boys, and that every woman's childhood is poisoned by "penis envy"! You may think that anyone who will believe that will believe anything, but I assure you, most of the child psychologists quite seriously do (and I think you're right), which is an indication of the lengths to which men will go in their refusal to believe that anything exclusively female could be paid the tribute of jealousy.

Now, men don't think they're superior because they really believe all this nonsense. On the contrary: they think all this nonsense because they really believe they are superior—first, I suppose, because of their horsepower; and later, I am positive, because there wasn't anything much around to read for centuries and centuries, but the Bible; the Epistles of St. Paul have always been men's favorite part of the Bible.

St. Paul is not my favorite saint, and I can't think why God didn't either fell him to the ground a great deal harder than He did or else set him to preaching, not Christianity but Judaism, which would have driven absolute *hordes* of Jews into the arms of the Church. St. Paul was not what you would call a winsome personality, even when he was a Jew. He did a lot of "breathing threats of slaughter against the disciples of the Lord" and taking out warrants for their arrest, for instance; but when it came to doing a little real *work*, like stoning St. Stephen, where do you find St. Paul? Standing around holding Stephen's cloak—in the shade, too, probably. After he was converted, though, Paul became impossible. He didn't give up persecuting, of course. But he turned his attention from Christians to women and he has had, in sum, a terribly bad influence on men ever since.

"Let a woman learn in silence, with all submission," St. Paul advised young Bishop Timothy, "for I do not allow a woman to teach or to exercise authority over man; but she is to keep quiet. For Adam was formed first, then Eve. And Adam was not deceived, but the woman was deceived and was in sin." Within a matter of days, without question, the men of Ephesus formulated that article of the male code of honor whose twentieth-century equivalent is: "I ain't taking no orders from no woman."

Today Ephesus; tomorrow the world.

Fifteen hundred years later, Queen Elizabeth, who was worth any 14 of the men she was addressing—and who knew it, what's more—felt she had to assure her troops that "I know I have the body of a weak and feeble woman, but I have the heart and stomach of a king, and of a king of England, too . . ." before she could proceed to the point, which was: I want you men to go out there and repel the army of Parma.

Women ought to keep their heads covered and men ought not, lovable old St. Paul wrote the Corinthians, because "a man is the image and glory of God. But woman is the glory of man. For man is not from woman, but woman from man [you see what *really* bothers men, don't you, the same thing that bothers three-year-old boys], for man was not created for woman, but woman for man. This is why the woman ought to have a sign of authority over her head." The men of Corinth—and of any other period or place you can think of— gave lovable old St. Paul a standing ovation before he had finished his first sentence and forthwith hastened out to pass his wisdom on to the *mores*-makers of the civilized world. Tennyson is the poet who is commonly considered to have given definitive expression to this thesis of St. Paul's—not presumably because it drove him to unprecedented heights of un-rhyme and un-rhythm, but because it inspired in him the requisite heights of un-reason.

"Man for the field and woman for the hearth," wrote the

parson's desk-bound son; "Man for the sword and for the needle she," proclaimed the ex-soldier who never met an enemy; "Man with the head and woman with the heart," declared the man who never could remember where he had lost his money and his manuscript; "Man to command and woman to obey," announced the in-and-out inmate of mental institution after mental institution; "All else confusion," concluded poor confused Alfred Lord Tennyson.

Today men who have never heard of either Tennyson or St. Paul paraphrase them with: "A man's gotta wear the pants of the family."

"Younger widows" (by which he meant any woman who was not under the direct supervision of a man), St. Paul warned, "being idle learn to go about from house to house and are not only idle, but gossipers as well, and busybodies, mentioning things they ought not." Men haven't stopped talking about how Women Talk Too Much since.

But St. Paul, like all of us, did have his softer moments. He freely conceded, for instance, that it is better to marry than to burn, though his personal advice to "the unmarried and to widows" was that "it is good for them if they so remain." And no one can deny that he made it more than easy to follow this advice. There is no telling how many Christian maidens decided to remain so after a long, cold look at St. Paul's contributions to the marriage ceremony. "Let women be subject to their husbands as to the Lord; because the husband is the head of the wife as Christ is the head of the Church . . . ," St. Paul briskly admonishes the bride before turning his attention to the young husband who, as a reasoning male, requires a little more delicate handling. "Husbands, love your wives, as Christ also loved the Church . . .so also ought men to love their wives as their own bodies. He that loveth his wife, loveth himself, for no man ever hateth his own flesh, but nourisheth it and cherisheth it." (Did some woman point this out to St. Paul?)

"For this cause shall a man . . . cleave to his wife; let everyone of you . . . love his wife as himself, and let the wife fear her husband."

Once this strongest of male motivations—"be good to your-self"—has been dangled as an inducement to husbandly love, the very least the bride can do, obviously, is to get lovable; and God's cooperation is forthwith requested to that purpose: ". . . May she be pleasing to her husband like Rachel; prudent like Rebecca; long-lived and faithful like Sara . . . may she fly all unlawful addresses and fortify her weakness by strong dis-cipline . . . be respected for her seriousness . . . venerated for her modesty . . . fruitful in offspring. May her life be pure and blameless . . . and may they both see their children's children unto the third and fourth generation and come at last to a happy old age."

You noticed when "she" turned into "they," didn't you? Just too late for the injunction and just in time for the reward which the old fool has earned, presumably by managing to love that paragon of virtue, his wife.

Well, if a virtuous woman is a crown to her husband, it's easy to see that there never has been, and never will be, a century of the common man.

So, Merry Christmas, all you kings. Happy New Year, all you virtuous women. I shall not ask *you* to be *my* valentine, St. Paul.

CHAPTER 20

Spare Me the Rods

In the late Fifties, the "New Math," as it was called, swept the educational system. Aloïse Heath, a veteran of multiplication tables, long division, fractions, ratio and proportion, through painful homework sessions with her older children, was now confronted with rods of different sizes and colors, the working tools of the New Math in kindergarten and grade school. Intrigued, ABH accompanies five-year-old Timothy to school to sit in on a math class. This piece, perhaps more than any other, illustrates her extraordinary ear for "child speak," and her absorbing interest in how a child's mind works.

The mother of a lot of scatterbrained, irresponsible, lazy little knuckleheads has much to be thankful for—the very, very least of which is that after ten or twelve years of driving children nightly to their desks; of finding, explaining, supervising, checking, and correcting homework, she finds that she, and she alone, has attained a good grammar school education.

She, and she alone, knows her multiplication tables—not only including, but especially, the eight times. She, and she alone, knows the name of the leader of the Jamestown Colony and the answer to what is Sanctifying Grace and three examples of subordinate clauses—begun by adjoining words—and the capital of Alaska. Only she knows the preamble to the Constitution by heart and the French for "*had I had time, I should have*

completed my assignment." Which is subjunctive, but not impossible. She is death on accidentals in the hard part of the
Moonlight Sonata, which is peachy, but not as ginger-peachy
as if one child ever remembered once about the G sharp in the
easy part.

This is why Timothy, who is the ninth of ten children, is
not over-protected by his mother. Timothy is five years old.
He is small, handsome, stern, rather conceited, we suspect; and
he has the kind of passion for accuracy which so unduly pro-
longs even the simplest of bedtime stories. When he comes
home from kindergarten, we meet; we do not re-une, as did
his poor bemomm̀ed eldest brother and I 12 years ago. Nor do
I ask for a detailed accounting of Timothy's morning; I say
"Have fun?" and then I say "That's good!" Sometimes I say
"That's good!" before he answers, and he has asked me not to.
I admire the drawings he brings home, but I do not frame
them.

Timothy was home from school today with a cold, and we
were glad to see each other, so to speak. We sat alone together
in the kitchen over a plateful of plums, and I said, as a gesture
of friendship: "Tim, what's two and two?" Between Heaths,
this is not a question; it is the opening gambit of an old routine
which ends in "What's 12 and 12?" to which the (always)
killingly funny answer is, "24. Shut your mouth and say no
more." Furthermore, it is Timothy's absolutely favorite joke;
so I felt a little rebuffed when he asked gravely:

"What's two?"

One's instinctive answer to a question like this is two is
two, dopey! But one does not give instinctive answers to questions posed by Timothy. Timothy has a tendency to pursue
questions right down through a crack in the floor. I decided
that what he meant was, Two whats?, so:

"Oh . . . plums," I told him.

Timothy studied his plum, which was purple. "When you

say plum do you mean puhple?" he asked hopefully. "Puhple is my favored."

It seemed to me that we were getting rather far afield. I said: "All right, purple. But I still want to know what two and two is."

"Brown," said Timothy; and then as I sat, open-mouthed: "BROWN is the ANSWER!" he repeated firmly.

Another clown in my family is very high on my list of what my family does not need; and I searched Tim's face for the slightest sign of a smirk while I groped my mental way back to the beginning of our conversation. There was no humor in either, I decided; and certainly there was no sense.

"Two and two is brown?" I asked at last.

"Puhple and puhple is brown," Timothy corrected. "It was you that said puhple."

Maternal masochism being what it is, I wiped the blood out of my eyes and staggered back into the ring. Where I learned— and it served me right—that two apples, two RED apples are purple, and two pears are orange. That is, two yellow pears are orange; two light green pears are, as anybody knows, dark green. ("Are you SMAHT?" Tim asked me curiously.) And one yellow pear and one green pear are, he was pretty sure, blue. Fighting back tears of sheer weakness, I finally took four oranges from the refrigerator and put them on the table. "Come on, now, Tim," I pleaded. "What are two oranges and two oranges, *orange* oranges?"

"Nothing," said Timothy flatly. He slipped off his chair with an air of finality. "Not even one ohnge and one ohnge is something. Don't you even know *that*?" and he started up the back stairs. "But, Tim," I called after him desperately. "You didn't even look at them! If there're two for you and two for . . ."

"Oh fouah!" he growled over his shoulder. "Fouah. Fouah. Fouah. Fouah. But Fouah is numbuhs. Kindagatuhs don't do numbuhs, I should hope." And he reached the top of the stairs and disappeared.

It was not till later that I realized that that silly secret language of the children's had something to do with substitut- ing colors for numbers, and that Timothy was becoming ob- sessed by it and that it must go.

After supper I went upstairs for a consultation with the joint rulers of the Lower Family, seven-year-old Betsey, who is very intellectual, and eight-year-old Alison, who is very wise. They were on the floor, in the Heath homework position—head down, rump up—and through each pair of rosy lips came inter- mittent mutters of "My God. My God." Blasphemy I can han- dle. I tip-toed into the room and applied a sharp smack to the high part of each little girl. Two dark heads shot up and two small faces blazed at me, but I got in the first word, which is important. "What did I hear you say?" I bellowed.

"My rods, my rods," said Betsey. "Shall we not any more?"

"Is it bad?" Alison asked interestedly.

This was obviously not my day. "Oh," I said weakly. "No, it's not bad. I thought you were saying something else . . ." ("My God," Alison whispered to Betsey.) "You each get a bad thing free, then." But I was still irritated, in general as well as in particular, and I added querulously: "It's idiotic, though. What do you mean, 'my rods'?"

"We have them at school," said Betsey.

"Well, what do you do with them, anyway?" I asked.

"Three-ninths times thirty-six equals box," said Alison.

"One quarter times box plus six equals box," said Betsey.

"With rods? Sticks?"

"Yes," they said.

I thought I'd better feel my way. "I used to do problems like that," I remarked, "but . . ."

"Do them, then," urged Alison. "Go on, Mother, let's see you do them." Gentle Betsey warned: "Mine is pretty hard, Mother."

So I did them, using partly common sense and partly x's; and I was very good about not telling them that these problems were different in degree of difficulty, but hardly at all in kind from those I had helped Jim and Pam and John with—not when they were seven and eight, but when they were thirteen.

"I don't say *box* though; I say *x*," I told them when I had finished.

"Didn't they even have rods in olden days?" Betsey asked, surprised.

"Well, pay attention then and I'll tell you," said Alison.

"And don't be afraid to ask questions," urged Betsey, and: "No, don't," added Alison. "You Can't Ask Questions Without Thinking," she announced magisterially, and, "There's No such Thing as Bad Thinking," she and Betsey chorused.

I thought I'd withhold comment on that one for a while, and I said:

"I will. I won't. I'll remember. Now tell me about the rods."

"Well. This is how I'd do three-ninths times thirty-six equals box with rods if I had my rods," said Alison. "They look like Lincoln logs except with edges, and they have ten sizes instead of four; and the biggest one is ten times as long as the littlest one. So first I have to see thirty-six; and I put three orange rods . . ."

"You forgot to *say* about colors," Betsey hissed.

"Okay, okay, *okay*, Betsey! Every size rod is a different color, so you can pick out the ones you want easier, I guess. The smallest one is white and the biggest one is orange and there's all different colors for the ones in between. See?"

I saw, I said.

"So the white rod is one and the red one is two and like that all the way up to the orange is ten. So if I *had* my rods I'd put three orange rods and one . . . Oh, by the way," Alison interrupted herself. "You *do* know that orange is only ten be-cause white is one, don't you? If I decided to call the white

rod a half, then the red would be one, and the green—that's
the next—would be one and a half and like that all the way
up to orange—that's the biggest, remember—would be five.
Or orange would be twenty if white was two. See?"

I saw, I said. It took me a moment but I saw. I saw something
else too, or I thought I did.

"Alison," I said, "I'm *very* interested. But before you go on:
Does Timothy have rods?"

"That's all poor Tim-Tim has," said Betsey.

"Well, then, tell me: if you were thinking about rods and
not about numbers, would you say that purple and purple is
brown?"

"Did he say that? That's pretty smart," said Alison admir-
ingly. "See, that's the same as four and four—purple's four:
white, red, green, purple; one, two, three, four—the same as
four and four is eight—unless you call purple eight and then . . ."

"It doesn't matter what you call it," said Betsey, quietly.
"Purple and purple is brown."

"And red and red is . . ."

"Purple."

"What's yellow and yellow?"

"Orange," said Betsey. "That's good if Tim-Tim said that."

". . . of course, I *could* make my first factor line with the
reds . . ." Alison was chattering on, unnoticing and unoffended;
and I finally did learn how she would have found out what
three-ninths of thirty-six are with her rods, if she'd had her
rods. I even *saw.*

And I'm sorry, but I think you should see, too, because it
was very interesting. Given the proximity of Alison and her
rods (which I just did) she would set end-to-end three orange,
or ten-count, and one dark green, or six-count rods, which
would give her 36. Then Alison would find nine rods of the
same color, or value, which, set end to end (or "added") along
her 36 row, would match it in length. These nine rods would

constitute a "factor line" for 36; as would any other series of rods of the same color which "fit." ("Like it would take 18 rods to fit the 36 line," Alison explained. "And red is two so you know one of the factors of 36 is 18 and another is two. See? And, when you find all the colors that fit, then you know all the factors.") Once she had found the rod which fit exactly nine times, she would know by its color, of course, what number it represented ("Four," I offered. "Purple," said Alison), and since nine purples ("Thanks, Mother, by the way") were nine-tenths of 40, and three purples were three-ninths of 36, and since purple was four, that was 12, and 12 was what you wrote in the box.

"It *says* longer than it *does*," finished Alison, "And of course it's much faster when you remember your factors."

"Couldn't you just use your nine times table?" I asked. "Or have you had that yet?"

"Oh, ye-a-ah! I've heard about those!" Alison sounded a little regretful. "We have factors though."

I thanked them very much; I told them to hurry to bed, it was late ("we've had some dumb old lady in here asking questions," Alison explained. "*Alison!*" said Betsey), kissed them goodnight and left. I felt better but all the same I got myself invited to kindergarten the next morning.

I arrive a few minutes late, which I assumed Timothy would expect, but I see in a moment both that he didn't and that he is in a state of high dudgeon. (I know most five-year-olds don't; but Timothy does.) Mrs. Lord, the kindergarten teacher, introduces me to the children as Timothy's mother while Tim tries to look as if you could knock *him* over with a feather and I say Good morning, and the children say Good morning, and You-Know-Who says mothers should go home, and we all settle down to a jolly arithmetic class.

On the children's low wooden tables, at which they sit in groups of two and three, are enormous numbers of brightly colored wooden "rods" of varying lengths; and these, I gather, are the tools of the famous M. Cuisenaire's mathematical rev-olution. Mrs. Lord explains to me hurriedly that the method of teaching arithmetic is to induce the children to make their own discoveries of basic mathematical patterns and facts; and that they are never discouraged, therefore, from voicing a conclu-sion, and never praised or reproached for being right or wrong.

"Heavens," I say. "What do you do with your face?"

"Practice," says Mrs. Lord and she leaves me to supervise Corky in the picking up of 14 small white rods which had suddenly and inexplicably risen from Corky's box and hurled themselves at Ricky's head. He thought it was odd at the time, Corky says, picking away slowly. Mrs. Lord doesn't wait. She assigns one of the longer rods to each of several children, and asks them to make "trains" or combinations of small rods to fit them. Bill, who has the orange rod, finds the most combina-tions, and he is awarded the honor of "reading" them aloud. He bends his head over his rods with enormous concentration and reads slowly: "Brown and red. Yellow, purple, white. Green, red, yellow."

"Good thinking, Bill," says Mrs. Lord, and she turns to the class. "Now suppose that orange rod that Bill found all those combinations for were a candy cane. And suppose Bill very nicely decided ..." ("Ha!" says someone, and I fear it is Timothy) "... to give me half of his candy cane. How much would he have left for himself do you think, if he did that?"

"Half a candy cane," cries half the class. "Half a candy cane," agrees Mrs. Lord. "A broken candy cane and I don't want it," Timothy observes pleasantly.

Mrs. Lord congratulates one and all on his keen perception, sound judgment and advanced intellectual development. She continues: "Some of you think that if Bill gives me half his candy cane what he'll have left is another half a candy cane. Does anybody disagree with that?"

Nobody disagrees with that, though Vanessa and Nancy confer.

"I wonder if any one can tell us how big the piece was that Bill gave to me. Vanessa?"

"*Half* big," says Vanessa firmly.

"I should hope," remarks Mary Sunshine Heath.

"And how big was the piece Bill kept? Nancy?"

"Half big too. Timothy Heath should hope," whoops Nancy collapsing into Vanessa's arms.

Only Mrs. Lord—Oh, admirable young woman—maintains her equanimity. When she can be heard, she says: "Good, Nancy. Now can anyone tell us why Bill's piece is half big too?"

"Andy?" says Mrs. Lord. Someone pokes Andy. "Yes?" asks Andy, who has been waving his hand in the air in order to give the impression that he is not listening to Corky. My cheeks ache for Mrs. Lord, as she repeats pleasantly: "If Bill gave me a piece that was half as big as his candy cane, how do we know that the piece he had left was also half as big as the candy cane?"

"Oh, but it had to be," Andy says earnestly. He pauses. "You see," he begins slowly, "if two people each get half a thing, that makes the whole thing. And halfs are as big as each other because—well, they're the same as each other. They even have the same name!" Andy puts his hands on his hips and glowers around the room. "Good thinking, Andy," says Mrs. Lord serenely. "Now let's go back to the candy cane," the teacher continues. "If the orange rod is the same as a whole candy cane, what do you think would be the same as half a candy cane?"

"Half an orange rod," cries the class, in happy unison.

"I don't want half a ohnge rod," says The Spirit of Christmas Future. "It tastes hohble!" and he looks around smugly, having once again *épaté les bourgeois*.

"Half an orange rod," smiles Mrs. Lord. "Good! Now does anybody think he can take that thought a little farther?" She glances from child to child; and there is silence. "Well, let's see what we can find out," she continues, "everybody take out an orange rod. Has everybody got his orange rod? Is that orange, Timothy? Get out your orange rod, Timothy."

Tim got out his orange rod, observing only that "puhple is puhtier."

"I want everyone to make a train to fit his orange rod, but use only yellow rods, for your train. Is everybody paying attention. Kathy, what did I say?"

As Mrs. Lord has correctly divined, Kathy hasn't the foggiest—the intellectual demands involved in stealing all one's tablemates' light green rods being what they are. However, one of the robbed obligingly hisses "yellow" and Kathy replies firmly: "Yellow, you said."

"Puhple, I said," says Old Sweetness and Light, but he places his two yellow rods end to end and lines them up alongside the orange.

In another moment, everyone except Kathy has finished his pattern; and a moment after that, Kathy unhurriedly pushes her second yellow rod into place under 13 pairs of waiting eyes.

"I BEAT!" shrieks Kathy.

The Spirit of Moscow takes place (or takes wing, according to the angle of your extremism) and Kathy is only with difficulty preserved from it. Furthermore, I am almost sure that Mrs. Lord has raised her voice—imperceptibly, to be sure; but definitely. Mrs. Lord never wants to hear the children shout and scream like that again. Why, Timothy's mother must think she's visiting a *nursery* class.

"No she doesn't. She thinks she's home," says Timothy clearly.

Eleven shocked and delighted little faces are turned toward Timothy's mother, who blushes.

Mrs. Lord clears her throat. "So we've all found out that
. . . how many yellows make orange? Donald?"

"Two!" shouts Donald, jumping to his feet. "I mean, two,"
he whispers subsiding.

"Is that true, everybody? Kathy? Clay? Ricky? Bill?"
Timothy is not asked and I silently congratulate the teacher
on having learned, in only black (7) weeks, that Timothy would
have answered: "Puhple."

It took me yellow years.

"So if the orange rod is the same as a whole candy cane,
what do you think is the same as half a candy cane?"

"Yellow!" the class roars.

"Who can say it for us, Ricky?"

Ricky jumps up and stands at attention and announces at
the top of his voice: "Yellow is one-half orange."

"One half is the yellow of orange," pipes Kathy.

"Two yellows make orange," says quiet Vanessa. "You have
to know that before the rest."

"You're quite right, Vanessa," says Mrs. Lord and she begins
to gather up her rods.

It is noon. The kindergarten day is over; and Timothy and
I walk out into the bright fall.

What had they learned, I wondered, these babies sixty and
sixty-five and seventy months old, in the half hour just past?

A great deal, it seemed to me. They did not learn that two
and two are four and half of four is two, which is like—but
not at all the same as—three and three are six and half of six
is three. Instead they discovered that yellow and yellow are
orange and that therefore, but not also, half of orange is yellow.
Soon they will know that orange can be called by the name
of any number within reach of their young minds.

This morning these children were brought to see the logic
of doubleness and halfness, which is a pretty big thing to

understand—at five, by making patterns with colored blocks; or at 14, by learning "x = 2y: y = ½x."

I wondered, too, if the New Mathematics, or the Modern Mathematics, is not simply the mathematical application of a very old science, called logic; and whether the "new" techniques of teaching are not as old as Socrates, helping the young men of Athens nearly twenty-five hundred years ago to stumble their wordy way toward eternal verities.

"Mother," Tim asked as we got into the car. "Was I good?"

"Good!" I said, "you were absolutely terrible."

"That's pretty good thinking, Mother, that's just how I was. I was absolutely tuhble," and a radiant smile lit up the dark little face. Whatever gets into Timothy had, once again, got out.

CHAPTER 21

It Says Here . . .

You know that house where, the night before Christmas, not a creature was stirring, not even a mouse? Well, that wasn't our house. That was a house where mamma in her kerchief and papa in his cap could settle their brains for a long winter's nap because they knew good and well that St. Nicholas was about to come down the chimney with a bound and do absolutely everything.

It may come as a surprise to many people, but the fact is, St. Nicholas doesn't do one blessed thing for the Heath family. At our house—and I wouldn't want this mentioned in front of just anybody—Santa Claus is really Ben and me; and the period during which not a creature is stirring, not even a mouse, lasts roughly from 4:10 to 5:00 A.M. By six o'clock, actually, you couldn't call what goes on in our house "stirring."

You know the family that gathers round the hearth on Christmas Eve while Father re-reads the beloved A Christmas Carol? Firelight flickering on absorbed little faces? Baby dropping off to sleep on Mother's shoulder? Well, that's not our family, and I bet you guessed.

I hope I'm not giving anyone the impression that Ben and I are not respecters of tradition, because the fact is that we're simply aslosh with traditions. We always sing Christmas carols after dinner; we always hang our stockings on the mantelpiece; we always set out cookies and milk for Santa Claus, but we just don't have the time to listen to Ben read *A Christmas Carol.* We have a substitute tradition: we give Janet and Timothy a half-teaspoon of liquid phenobarbital, Jennifer, Betsey, and Alison a teaspoon, and Buckley, Priscilla, and John two teaspoons each. (We've had to keep the two eldest off the stuff these past two years; they have to stay alert.)

Then we send 16-year-old Jim, who has a voice like a bull calf, into the living-room with the big children and make *him* read Dickens' beloved *A Christmas Carol*; and 14-year-old Pam, who has such a sharp eye and a quick hand that she can whack a small bottom while its owner is still wondering which trespass to commit, takes the peewees into the nursery to hear Clement C. Moore's beloved "A Visit from St. Nicholas."

Ben and I refill the coffee pot and proceed forthwith to the furnace room, which is where *we* spend Christmas Eve. Not by choice, you understand—if we had a choice we'd watch *Amahl and the Night Visitors* or take a walk or something—but because the furnace room is the only one in our house in which you can a) store 167 different items, ranging from aeroplane: gasoline-powered to Zig-Zag Puzzle Map; and also b) lock.

Nine out of ten of these items, you understand, have to be organized or set up, or assembled, and a good many of them have to be either re-constructed or re-designed from scratch. All of them must be fully understood if Christmas morning is not to shrill with the sad cry of: "What's all that stuff supposed to *be?*" and "The box says Astro-Dyno Jet, but it's just a bunch of iron sticks!" or "I'll never be able to play that. The directions have too long words." All of which leaves Ben and me with the choice of working in the living-room after the last child is asleep—and when you have ten children that means never—or spending Christmas Eve in the furnace room.

The furnace room is rather peaceful, actually. By the time we've opened the boxes and laid out the hammer, saw, screwdrivers, wrenches, pliers, files, glue, rubber cement, safety pins, needles and thread, toothpicks for stiffening tabs that won't go into slots, crochet hooks and rubber bands for putting dolls' arms back on, Mercurochrome, Band-Aids, tranquilizers, Benzedrine, phenobarbital, aspirin, and a dictionary, we hardly even notice the furnace which has a way of breathing like a dinosaur with croup. Jim's voice, bellowing "Sit DOWN, Buckley," or "I said QUIET," filters down to us in a soft murmur; and since the nursery is on the third floor and Pam's energy is limited, she only clatters down every now and then to tell us that Alison is blowing into Jay's ear and blaming it on Betsey, or that Alison keeps sticking her feet under Timothy and pinching him with her toes, or that Alison keeps muttering "moon on the *breast* of the new-fallen snow, moon on the *breast* of the new-fallen snow" and making all the others laugh and act silly . . . "Well, she *thinks* it's a bad word, Mother, or she wouldn't bother to say it. You know how absolutely vulgar Alison is."

"Send her down to Jim's group," I roar through the screws in my mouth, which isn't much help—or much help to Jim, anyway—but my maternal instinct always seems to wane as my mechanical instinct waxes.

If you could call it an instinct.

If you could call it mechanical.

I do know some of my limitations, though, so I always start with a simple thing, like "ROLLING TENNIS: A new game for home fun," for instance. ROLLING TENNIS only has about six pieces, which is practically boring to a woman who was on Dean's List the entire first semester of her sophomore year at college. The instructions are nice and short, too. *The elastic steel needle,* they begin . . . (There's no elastic steel needle in the box, but the nearest thing to it is a kind of hard, spiky thing that bends, so that must be what) *must be kept in a way that it sits up on the edge of the table.* The trouble is, it won't stay in a way that it sits up on the edge of the table unless I hold it there, and surely the ROLLING TENNIS people couldn't mean that, could they? They don't really mean for me to spend the declining years of my life holding up that spiky thing! Do they realize that I have ten children? That I'm 43 years old? Well, of course they do. There's some perfectly simple thing that I've overlooked.

"Ben, it says here . . . " I begin.

"First things first," mumbles Ben, who is engaged in his annual reestablishment of diplomatic relations with the electric train, which he always can't understand something in the trans-former of. I don't tell him that if he'd leave the train up all year round he and the transformer wouldn't have to go through this every Christmas Eve. I don't tell him because it's too early. This is what I tell him around 2:00 A.M., and I'm a stickler for tradition.

Anyway, it's time to check everybody's teeth (and to tell Alison for the last time that sticking her toothbrush under the faucet doesn't fool *me* for one minute) and to hear everybody's prayers (and to tell Alison for the last time that beating every-body else to the "Amen" is *not* praying) and to kiss everybody goodnight (and to kiss Alison twice and tell her I love her anyway, which is the simple truth). On my way down I hear the baby calling "H-e-ere, Mudda! Here, boy! *Come* on!" and since I am training her in obedience—you can never begin too young, I always think—I obey, and we have a little chat and a little rock and a little back rub until she falls asleep again.

By the time I get back to the furnace room Ben has had time to accomplish a great deal, and I feel much better about every-thing, even ROLLING TENNIS.

So, all right, I will hold the spiky thing in a way that it sits up on the edge of the table. It's not as if the children were going to play rolling tennis eight hours a day! Now: *By a slight pressure of this needle upon the axis of the runner fitted with a rubber tie the latter one begins to move, the other player swiftly catches, stops it to run and jerks back with the same movement.*

Only there's no runner. There is a rod with a little rubber tire at each end, but if that's the runner, how would I press its axis? Anyhow, an axis is what things *turn* on, isn't it? I know it is; I won't even look it up; and it's nine o'clock and Ben has started to fiddle with that idiotic transformer again. ROLLING TENNIS will simply have to wait till he finishes. At least I know the rules. *He who has won a point plays last, but in a new game it is the last loser who plays first.*

I pull out Your Friendly Corner Store. This is more my type, and besides it has a diagram which not only illustrates and labels Parts A to X of the Corner Store, but also its accessories. "Telephone," it tells you, under a picture of a telephone. "Cord." "Cash register." "Your Friendly Corner Store sign."

"Check off each step as you complete it," they warn you (and show you how—like this ☒) and "Follow all directions step by step." I never was a leader, anyhow, so I start right in. *Step 1.* ☐ *From the white side of the board press out all excess fireboard from all slots, notches and edges so that all the parts look like those in the kit drawings.* ☐ *Punch out holes for screws with a sharp pencil point.* ☐ *Place parts in alphabetic order.* My Friendly Corner Store and I are not so friendly as we used to be, by the time I finish Step 1. I feel they have been not quite straight with me. They clearly implied that there was only one ☐ to a step, but, I now note, there are seven ☐'s in step 10, alone.

"Ben, look at this. It says here . . ."

"There's no point in getting mad about it," says Ben, who has made up with the transformer, solved ROLLING TENNIS (they meant "axle," not "axis," if that means anything to you) and is happily assembling some Thermo-Turbo thing without so much as a glance at the directions.

"Who's mad?" I snarl. Setting up the Corner Store involves

pushing 78 stupid little slots, and I know from experience that at the slightest sign of irritation on my part the tabs will turn into 78 sulky little bits of tissue paper. I grit my teeth and plod on. By the time I finish Step 12 (49 □'s later) Ben has put together the bicycle, the tricycle, the tractor, both doll carriages, the doll's house and the Walker Wagon. He is about to begin the electric hockey game when he discovers the instructions are in French. He hands me the instructions.

I can read French all right, but who knows what a *filet des buts* is, for heaven's sake, or a *casier pour pile sèche*, or a *vis à métal*, except maybe a French electrician. I go upstairs for the Larousse. (*I* know; but I don't think a French dictionary should necessarily be an integral part of Christmas Eve, not even at our house.) When I let myself back into the furnace room Ben looks at me for the first time this evening and blanches.

"Are you going to church like that?"

"Like what?" I answer huffily. And rhetorically.

Ben holds the Dreamy Dressing Table mirror up to my face. "It's 11:30," he says, and I tear up the stairs again.

Midnight Mass clears the crossness out of me. Priscilla goes with us this year, along with John and Pam and Jim; and as I watch them come back from Communion they look so solemn and young and tired and beautiful that my heart almost bursts. My heart almost bursts until I kiss them "Merry Christmas" in the cold starlight outside the church, and they refuse, with cries of revulsion, to kiss each other. Then my heart shrivels right back to normal.

Still, the furnace room *is* an anti-climax.

By 1:30, Ben and I are getting ruthless. When we find that the assembly instructions for John's cuckoo clock take up a 16-page booklet and begin: "Look what we have here!! What fun!! It's all the parts that go to make a real-as-life BLACK FOREST CUCKOO CLOCK!!" we clap the cover right back on the box and agree to pretend we thought he wanted a do-it-yourself cuckoo clock. We give up on the Corner Store after we notice that, besides the 19 Steps on the front of the instruction sheet, there are an additional 33 on the back. Anyhow, Betsey hasn't mentioned that Corner Store in weeks.

By 2:15 the B-52 Turret Gun, the Helicopter-Bomber, the Kookie Kitchen, the weight-lifting set and the puppet theater are assembled and upstairs; by 3:00 we've finished the musical rocking chair, the robot lady, the Sonar set, the fire engine, the weather station, the Yakkity-Yob, and we've even found out how to make the Kissy dolls kiss. By 3:45 every last item is complete and in the living-room; the Christmas list has been recovered from the rubble on the furnace room floor, and we're ready to distribute. That is, Ben arranges artistic exhibits and I sit on the floor stuffing Christmas stockings and tell him where artistically to arrange them.

"No, not there, honey: the Winchester rifle is Alison's. Put it on the desk with the Hedda-Get-Bedda doll . . . That Chubby Checker album goes with Pam's stuff, Ben. Right over there— by the lounging pyjamas. The Mass in B Minor is John's—in the corner, sweetie! With the lie detector and the minerology set." Or: ". . . Ben, he's not even four years old! And anyhow, couldn't we thrash this out some other time? . . . All right, all right, but just for now would you please put that Kissy doll under the piano with Timothy's dump truck?"

And finally we're through. We thumbtack a sheet across the entrance to the living-room and tiptoe upstairs to hang stockings on children's bedposts. Ben takes those for the children who don't believe in Santa Claus, because if they wake up they'll know it's only Daddy with the stockings; and I take those for the children who do, because if they wake up, they'll know it's only Mother.

At 4:10, in the black dark of the upstairs hall, I tiptoe round a corner into Ben, tiptoeing from the opposite direction. I gasp and clutch him.

"It's only Santa Claus."

"Oh, Ben," I sigh, too tired even to move away from his cheek, which feels like a cactus patch. "What will we ever do when the children are grown up?"

CHAPTER 22

Politics and Mortal Sin

Intensely interested in politics, ABH became a committed conservative after a youthful indiscretion. In 1936 she marched in a pro-FDR rally at Smith College, which resulted in a black eye when an infuriated Landon supporter tried to wrest away her banner. (The episode gave birth to a ditty: "One eye black/ And one eye gray/ How did Allie/ get that way?/ Allie was a Democrat/ Met a Rep/ Who was a rat/ And he/ Gave her/ A swell/ Shiner.") In 1964 she campaigned vigorously for Barry Goldwater, as did the children, including Janet, the baby, who was five. Goldwater's nomination had torn the Republican Party in two. The politicians mentioned in this story are Senator Kenneth Keating, Republican of New York, a onetime conservative favorite for revealing that Khrushchev had installed missiles in Cuba several weeks before JFK discovered them there. But Keating was now in disfavor, having refused to support the Goldwater campaign and blocked the effort to get the Goldwater–Bill Miller ticket on the Conservative Party line in New York. Senator John Tower of Texas was the first Republican to be elected (1961) to the Senate in the deep South, but he was considered insufficiently supportive of Goldwater's campaign, at least by the Heath children, to whom 99.99 per cent pure was not pure enough. Senator Strom Thurmond of South Carolina became the first prominent Southern senator to switch from the Democratic to the Republican Party, in the summer of 1964. Madame Nhu's husband, the

brother of South Vietnam's President Ngo Dinh Diem, was
killed in the coup that overthrew Diem. The coup was believed
to have been authorized by President Kennedy, whose own assas-
sination followed Diem's by a couple of weeks.

Every year about this time a dear man to whom I am closely
related by marriage (and to whom procrastination, needless to
say, is not a pressing personal problem) composes his annual
list of seventy-five or eighty New Year's resolutions which, if
I only stick to them this time . . . The truth is that if I only
stick to them this time, I assure you, I will be dead by May.
("There was nothing I could do," Dr. Nichols will tell my
grieving family. "She simply lacked the will to live.")

Ben doesn't believe I would be dead by May. Well . . . good
heavens, I *trust* he doesn't! No, of course he doesn't: What he
thinks is that I'll be perfect by May if I would, just for once,
cut out all those silly political meetings at night so that I would
joyously jump out of bed at 6:45 every morning and, all aglow
from my isometric exercises and my hot and cold shower and
my decent-breakfast-for-a-change, *drive* the children to school
instead of spending a lot of money I don't have on the school
bus. Also cut out all those silly political phone calls that keep
me glued to a chair 12 hours a day instead of keeping the
children's rooms and drawers and shelves and closets and desks
and toy chest tidy so as to teach them neatness by example if
I can't do it any other way and stop spending a lot of money
I don't have buying a child new undershirts because the storage
room is in such a mess I can't find the undershirts the next
child up outgrew last spring. Also cut out subscribing to all
those silly political publications that do nothing but make a
shambles out of my desk, and stop donating a lot of money I
don't have to any two-bit political outfit that asks me to; and
then when I go hog wild over birthdays and Christmas at least
I'd have a little cash to do it with. Also, cut out all those silly

political talks I'm everlastingly having with some child who should have been in bed hours ago, instead of supervising his practicing and checking his homework for that expensive edu-cation I am spending a lot of money I don't have for. And solemnly resolve to cut out all that political stuff once and for all and pay some attention to my family for a change.

Now that's Ben's idea of the perfect woman, nobly planned. My own is on a vastly higher, more spiritual scale, and far, far more reachable, which is just as well, because it is even more emetic. Some day, though, I *will* have a fling at becoming a perfect woman, nobly planned, which, the way I dope it out, means spending absolutely hours making love your whole exis-tence, and keeping silent in the churches, and weeping while men work, and trying to be a better smoke than a good cigar and constantly widening the gap between your price and rubies', and being good and letting who will be clever, and while your babies around you cling showing Wordsworth how divine a thing a woman may be made.

In my case, though, it will have to be while my grandbabes around me cling, because right now, and for the next 14 and a quarter years, I'm going to be too busy.

What's taking all my time right now is nobly planning my children. As a matter of fact it's a Thirty-Year Noble Plan and I am roughly 15 and three-quarter years along on it. (Thirty is not an arbitrary figure, by the way: it's the time it takes ten children to get from kindergarten to college if the last was born fourteen years after the first.) The object of my Thirty-Year Plan is to teach all the children exactly What to Think, and if they can't to ask their dear Mother, who does.

Call me a flawed woman, vulgarly planned, but call me not a lazy flawed woman, vulgarly planned—or at least not until you have meditated awhile on the exigencies of teaching any-thing, let alone What to Think, to ten children who include both a college freshman with sensory perception (it's not so much what the guy *says*; it's what he *exudes*. You know that ACLU-SANE Nuclear Policy miasma? Maple-flavored?) and a kindergartner of unshakable opinion (what we can't shake in Janet is her firm opinion announced thirty seconds after she heard of the President's assassination last year that Senator Goldwater shot him. "Janet, you *mustn't* say that!" her horrified older brothers and sisters exclaim when the subject comes up from time to time. "I won't. I won't tell *anyone*," she reassures them. "Shall it be our two's secret?" What I think is that for 49 months of age the child showed an extraordinarily astute nose for politics).

I started my little educational program when I was the un-sophisticated young mother of a lone kindergartner along about the time the pterodactyls were thinning out. Jim came home from school one day and self-consciously handed me a sheet of paper scratched up with a brown and a red crayon. "Look at my beautiful cow," he said with a syrupy smile. We stared at each other, wide-eyed, across the paper, each knowing that the other knew perfectly well that Jim didn't for one moment think that was a picture of a cow; he thought it was what it was, a bunch of scribble-scrabble in brown and red.

"Oh, come on, Jim," I said finally. He giggled and shrugged his shoulders. "Miss Betty said it was a cow first," he explained a little defiantly. "It was drawing time and I didn't want to draw so I played with a toy cow that's there, instead, and sometimes I made some marks with a crayon so she'd think I *was* drawing. And then pretty soon Miss Betty came and she said, 'Oh, *Jimmee*, I *like* your cow,' and I thought she meant the cow in my hand, but she didn't, she meant my scribble-scrab-ble. Isn't she crazy, Mother?"

And she was, of course, as I found out, but not more crazy than she had been taught to be and studied very hard to become. "I *wish* you hadn't discouraged him," she said mournfully a few days later. "Whatever he said when he came home, your little boy really and truly did draw a cow the other day but it was a cow as he sees cows, not as some adult has forced him to see a cow. What your little Jimmee brought you was very precious—it was, you might say, the essence of cowness as cowness appears to the unspoiled little soul God gave to Jim." And more, much more. I listened to all of it and thanked her politely and I drove straight home muttering, "Garbage. Garbage. Garbage. Garbage," for the whole 12 miles. When I got home I told Jim I wanted to talk to him and we sat on the porch steps and I asked him to sing me *Jingle Bells*. He looked a little puzzled but he sang it all the way through in two-four time in the key of G—observing half-notes, quarter-notes, whole notes and rests. He sang B-notes where B-notes occur in the song and D-notes where D-notes occur and he sang them in the octaves in which they were written. He sang it all the way through, ending squarely on the G above middle C and he held the G for an additional count of three before he closed his mouth, swallowed, and looked up at me, and I swallowed too and kissed him and told him he was wonderful. Then I hummed *Three Blind Mice* and asked him (though I already knew) if he could sing *Jingle Bells* that way in school. "Of course not," he said. "Why not?" I asked. He thought for a while and then he said slowly that if you sing one song instead of another you just aren't singing that first song. So then I thought he was ready for the first lesson in What to Think and we decided that scribble-scrabble could be designs but they couldn't be cows, and pictures of cows could be called cows even if they aren't very good but if they were pink and had three legs and two tails, you couldn't call them just cows. You had to call them pretend cows or funny cows because that was what was true about them.

Well, he wasn't about to become a Picasso naturally. For years and years after that, while the teachers told me that their job was to teach a child How to Think, not What to Think lest their brains wouldn't develop and they would never build up any mental muscles, I busily filled the young heads with the What that the school disapproved of so highly. For I had visions of my ten grown into handsome young people twenty years hence, sitting around flexing and unflexing their mental muscles because no one had remembered to put anything inside their heads to give the muscles a workout.

It's only 14 years later, but still I think you would agree I've done a moderately extreme job. Drop in at our house some snowy afternoon this Christmas. Take that big old chair under the lamp. Stretch your feet out to the fire—you must be freezing. The children are all in the kitchen making cocoa. They are going to bring their mugs in here and toast marshmallows to go with it. Shall I have them bring a cup for you? Coffee then: or would you rather have a drink to warm you up?

I wonder if I can ask you to be quite frank with me. Are you tired, edgy, wrought-up? Do you start at sudden noises, and cringe at shrill sounds? Have the holidays turned you into a walking bundle of raw, quivering nerves? If so, would you tell me and I'll have the children stay in the kitchen with their cocoa. Please do be frank. I mean it. You don't know what they can do to you. They are all so noisy—even as individuals they are noisy—and they never get off the subject of politics.

What crowd noise? You mean the football game on television? Oh, that crowd noise! Well, that's what I was trying to tell you, that's the children.

I think I'll just fix you a drink anyway . . . a double, maybe . . . because in just about twenty seconds that door across the hall will explode open with the force of—well, not an atomic bomb, but certainly one of the old TNTs—and hit the wall with a shotgun blast, and, following a brief flurry of growls and snarls as two and a half times more Heaths than will fit try to get through the doorway first, twenty young feet will blump heavily across the hall and the living room and ten raucous young voices will continue whatever political (it's always political) argument (it's always an argument) they have been having.

"Listen, Buster," Jim will bellow with whatever God put in his neck instead of vocal cords, "in 1960, I was 15 years old, as old as you are now! I *heard* Nixon with my own ears and, for your information, it took Kennedy to make him sound like a conservative. And I mean, it took everything Kennedy had!"

"Hold it, *hold it*, HOLD IT!" John squeaks, which happens when he pushes too hard (he will croak the next sentence because his voice is apparently changing on a ten-year plan). "In the first place I happened to be 11 and a half years old in that election and I don't exactly think Donald Duck was running against Popeye! But what I'm talking about is a man can grow, can't he? *This* election, Nixon sounded more like Goldwater than Goldwater did!"

"Of course, I've always liked Towers of Texas," 13-year-old Priscilla inserts priggishly into the pause—very quickly because in our family there is a great deal of competition for pauses. She gives Pam, who is 17, and her idol, a quick sidelong glance to see whether she has noticed that what Priscilla has just said was repeated word for word from what Pam said at lunch. She's in luck; only her Mother has noticed it.

"Tower, you fink, not Towers," one of the boys growls.

"She means she likes all the Towers," says Alison, whose position as undisputed boss of the five younger children has given her perhaps a slightly exaggerated sense of security. The peewees laugh—a little too heartily—as they do at all sallies directed against the family teenagers.

The children have settled themselves and their mugs around the fireplace and one by one they will discover you sitting half hidden in the big chair. A stricken look briefly crosses every face but little Janet's but you will not notice; because you,

POLITICS AND MORTAL SIN

even as I, are watching with alarm mounting to panic, the spectacle of ten clumsy young things struggling to their feet from the midst of ten tall, tippable mugs of cocoa.

"Don't get up!" we cry in chorus and the children settle back and acknowledge their introductions with little ducks and nods of the head like reporters on "Meet the Press." Janet is already on the arm of your chair and turning her face towards yours. She will examine you carefully while the rest of the family holds its breath in anticipation of Janet's terrible personal remarks. This time she spares us. There are apparently more important things on her mind. "Where is your button?" she says. "How can I know who you are for?" You look at me inquiringly and I explain: "Janet hasn't accepted the mandate of the people. In fact, she's turned it down and she's resumed her campaign for Goldwater."

"Oh," you say, "I see! You mean that button!" and you slip a hand into your pocket. "Why do you keep saying so many things and the thing I asked you to say is who are you for?" Janet asks again. "Senator Goldwater, of course," you assure her solemnly. "Good for you," Janet will crow, patting your head. Then she leans down toward the hearth and shrills, "Hey, you guys," to the group sitting below her, but the atmosphere has changed down there. The battle lines have been drawn and the troops drawn up over the question of whether Senator Keating or Senator Thurmond had behaved the worst, considered from the standpoint of his own party. Buckley, Alison, Betsey, Jennifer and Timothy are firmly ranged against Senator Thurmond and their elders, and so is Priscilla really, but she does not participate because she cannot bear to be against Pam.

The three big children from the pro-Thurmond group and the boys, belying the maturity they so often remind me of, are behaving badly indeed. Pink with rage and their blue eyes bulging, they shout insults at the huddled little group across the hearth. "You stupid little baby finks. Don't you know *any-thing!* When we were your age . . ." There is a pause while Jim considers whose age he is talking about and in the silence Betsey's composed little voice rings out. "Mother," she says through the long black braids she is tying under her nose, "will you explain to those guys over there that a whole traitor is worse than half a traitor? And will you ask them please if they can figure out whether Keating or Thurmond was the whole traitor?"

The insult is grave and Betsey's cool little face is so unbear-ably smug that I can feel my own palms itching. I can under-stand the double-decibel value of the resulting pandemonium. John's eyes, though, have turned from gray to sky-blue—always a danger signal, and when I see his hand creep toward one of the gooier marshmallows I know *exactly* what he has in mind. I jump to my feet, clapping my hands together so hard they still sting an hour later; and I roar: "That's e-NOUGH!" Through the sudden silence Janet's little voice comes sweetly. She is addressing you. "Do you want to hear something bad about Mother?" This puts you, I can see, in a difficult position so I nod reassuringly. "Yes, I'd love to," you tell Janet. "Well," she confides, but by no means in a confidential tone, "Mother won't let me say the President is a poo-poo. And he is!" I look down at the hearth where, the fight forgotten, the older children are holding their mouths and rolling back and forth in sheer plea-sure. You raise your eyes in inquiry and I am able to say quite truthfully, "I have no idea what she means." In 19 years of motherhood I have successfully kept from knowing what a poo-poo is and don't think it's been easy but moments like this are the reward of my firm refusal to increase my vocabulary.

Nevertheless, the situation is infuriating and I suggest as I certainly would not have if I had thought twice, "Priscilla and Buckley, why don't you sing your new song for us?" They both flush with pleasure, having had no compliments to date on their song, and sit down at the piano. This is your lucky day. You are about to hear an original poem set to the music of the enchanting old melody *Chopsticks*. Priscilla and Buckley play an introductory two measures and then the "girl" verses, composed and sung by Priscilla, begin:

> *Two young brides of yesteryear*
> *Are now two widows sad-ad-ad.*

(All right: you're singing a poem to *Chopsticks*.) The Buckley, or boy verses, are sung with his choirboy sweetness and charm, as indeed they need to be:

> *Diem, the husband of Mme. Nhu*
> *Got stabbed to death with You, You, You*
> *Know it hurts a lot*
> *President Kennedy got shot*

The moral of the poem seems to be that if Kennedy had managed to save Diem, Oswald would have been just one more spectator along the presidential parade route in Dallas.

Well, they are only 13 and eleven. Forgive them.

Six-year-old Timothy, who has been standing aloofly in the background watching you with great concentration, has apparently now accepted you. He whispers in my ear that he has something important to tell here. I transmit the message and Timothy stands before you shortly and informs you somberly that his message is about Communism. The Communists, he thinks you ought to know, are against us and we are against Communists, and they plan to beat us up but, man, are they going to be surprised, because they don't even *know* about Timothy Heath yet! And with modest pride, Terrible Timothy sticks one skinny little leg in the air and shows you his heavy brace and boot. "One kick with *that* foot," he grits from clenched teeth, and while you ponder the appalling fate in store for the Communists, Tim smiles and the serious little face breaks into whole galaxies of twinkles and dimples.

Tim-Tim, like all the children, is An Authority. Ask them about the Congo or Katanga. Or Vietnam. (Mme. Nhu is a sub-specialty, exclusive rights to which are held by Priscilla Heath.) But ask her anything. Oh, and Pete Seeger. Ask them anything about Pete Seeger. (He was at college with Jim for a while but he returned just last night.)

No, don't ask us about the Warren Report for yet a while. The three big children are trying to stick their loving Mother with it and I can't thrash the matter out with them until after Christmas (I do think drawing straws is the only fair way).

Buckley has exclusive rights to the Hungarian Freedom Fighters till next term when they will be transferred to John for a paper. Pam is our propaganda specialist. Ask her what two words the press used to beat Goldwater. As a matter of fact I'll tell you now. One word was "tried" and the other was "claimed." The press always reported Johnson as having stated "x" or denied "x," but Goldwater, on the other hand, invariably claimed "x," or tried to deny "x." Pam's parlor game is to invent phrases, like "he found the diamond" to put after the two positive statements, and "he stole the diamond" to be used after the two negative statements.

But go on. Ask her anyway.

Janet, by this time, has shinnied all the way up your leg and arm to your shoulder. She grasps your chin with a firm little hand and is turning your head towards her bright little monkey face. She asks you twice, breathlessly, "You know what!" Assuming that you do not, she now tells you with an expression of great ferocity that she is not just only going to kick those *Commonists*, like Tim-Tim. She is going to kill them. Dead, she adds, like *this* and she demonstrates what seems to be execution by a single body blow of unbearable drive and power. Then, quite possibly, she will spit.

And I *do* hope she misses you—tsk, tsk, oh, that beautiful sports jacket (Jennifer, run get a cloth)—and after you have been so sweet and patient listening to all these children! But I told you, remember? This is why Ben spends Sunday afternoon locked in his bedroom with the television set. Lovely to have seen you.

Oh, there's a question you wanted to ask me before you go? Did I *really* tell Tim-Tim that Tommy Major's mother was going to Hell because she voted for Johnson? No, I DID NOT. Once and for all.

What happened was this. One day Timothy said: "Would you go to Hell if you voted for Johnson?"

I said: "Do you mean me or do you mean people? If you mean me, the answer is yes because I'm an educated voter and I'd be committing a mortal sin if I voted for him. If you mean 'people,' no, because they are not as smart as your dear, dear mother, you lucky boy." Tim looked at me gravely. "Will Tommy's mother go to Hell? She's going to vote for Johnson."

"Oh, I don't think so, Tim," I said, not terribly interested in the whole subject. "She doesn't know enough to know what she's voting before. But wouldn't she be surprised if she *did* go to Hell!"

It was then that I made my big mistake. You remember those lovely warm days last fall. Well, they affect me very badly. They increase my euphoria to the point of mania. I was near the piano while I talked to Tim and I sat down and played and sang, "*Tommy's mother went to Hell/ On the Donkey ticket/ Now she knows a Johnson vote/ Is very, very wicked.*" Timothy thought it was charming and rushed out to collect his friends Brian and Billy to hear it. Billy called in his sister Beth, who was playing with Pammy Shepherd from the next street over. In about ten minutes there were over a dozen children in the

house bawling out at the top of their lungs the news that
"*Tommy's mother went to Hell.*" And what was I doing? Big
fat fool that I am. I was sitting there at the piano bawling it
out with them and playing different versions of the piano
accompaniment and setting up duets and interesting arrangements and in general behaving not at all like a woman whose
living room windows face onto the Major driveway. And that's
absolutely all there is to it.

I don't blame her for thinking it was a rehearsal. I don't
even blame the children for telephoning her the next few days
and nights to sing it. I drummed it into their heads so hard
they probably still can't think of another tune. And that I
swear is the whole story. It is absolutely what happened. And
don't believe any other version.

And we *do* speak.

CHAPTER 23

A Heath
Christmas Carol Program

Ｎone of the Heath children was born on Sunday, but many of them almost were, which may account for the fact that, although bright *and* bonny *and* good *and* gay they are not, bonny and gay they indubitably are.

They may get A2 in handwriting and D4 in word analysis; they may get "whole-heartedly enthusiastic" in sports and "constantly inattentive" in social studies, but they are the bonniest crew—not in the whole country; that's ridiculous, I always tell people—in New England. Though, I admit it, I don't know the rest of the country very well.

It is regrettably true that they forge their father's name to undone homework slips (remember those A's in penmanship) at eight; that they fall in love with and torture members of the opposite sex at 11; and that by the age of 12 they have discovered that you can smoke into the exhaust fan of the first-floor lavatory with absolute safety, whereas smoking out of the third-floor bathroom means Mother calls the Fire Department. (They learn about cigarettes young because when we catch them smoking, we beat them.)

And gay my children unquestionably are. They rollick into the house from school, burst into paroxysms of laughter at the extraordinary coincidence of their reunion from various carpools, plan their far-flung wickednesses in gales of muffled giggles, are scolded with eyes twinkling above insufficiently suppressed grins, and fall asleep in the midst of a choked chuckle at 8, 9, or 10 P.M., according to whether their bedtime was at 7, 8, or 9 P.M.

And they sing! Lord, how they sing! They sing alone or in unison, in harmony, cacophony, or competition, and if two of the stubborn ones simultaneously embark on "The Surrey with the Fringe on Top," and "Silent Night," an immediate popularity contest ensues, as other children drift into the room and join in one song or the other. If the singers are equally popular, you just have to break it up. (Not by saying: "Break it up," you understand. Who's listening? What I usually do is play "The Stars and Stripes Forever" very loudly on the piano.)

With all the gaiety and caroling that goes on in our house all year round, it is only natural that we plan, early every December, a Christmas carol program to put on tape after it is absolutely perfect, and send to the children's grandmother as an absolutely unique, unprocurable in stores, Christmas gift.

One reason this always seems feasible in early December is that around then the children are infinitesimally better-behaved than usual. I myself attribute this to the fact that their father and I are infinitesimally worse. I have even discussed with Ben the potentialities of our being worse all the time, for the children's own good, but he insists he is the same at Christmas time as he is the year round, which, as I occasionally—well, maybe a *little* more often than occasionally—point out, is a clear admission that he is impossible all the time.

In any case, there's no question that, around Christmas time, the children are more cooperative. All of them will stand still and concentrate, instead of two reading comic books and three wrestling under the piano. They willingly all sing "fa-la-la-la-la, la la! la! la!," even though most of the boys, and all of the girls under 12, say it makes them feel silly. All in all, it seems an ideal time to plan a Christmas program, and I do so, in spite of a) an unbroken record of failure, and b) the boys.

Boys, as anyone with fewer resources than the director of the Vienna Boys' Choir knows, are an insuperable obstacle to group singing. I am convinced that Madame von Trapp had hers wired for sound.

In our family, 21-year-old Jim is the only dependable boy. He has a soft, melodious tenor voice, he sings fa-la-la without shame, and he whacks the little ones when they fidget. Seventeen-year-old John, who also has a nice voice, is, unfortunately, musically gifted, and refuses to waste his talent on mere singing. He plays the descant to the carols on his recorder, and if there is not a satisfactory descant he composes one, which is lovely, but it leaves Jim alone and lonely down there below middle C. Buckley, at 13, sings a high and piercingly sweet soprano, but he is under the impression that a listening world will believe his voice has changed if he emits all sounds an octave lower than is normal to him. And he sings that way until his ribs are so sore from his brothers' and sisters' pounding that he can barely sing at all, which, as I keep pointing out, may be good for discipline, but not for Christmas carol programs. Timothy, who is a crotchety eight, refuses flatly to make any concessions on the part of the language as it is spoken, to the language as it is sung. "Glo-o-o-o, o-o-o-o-o, o-o-o-o-o-oria" is not for Tim. He sings "Glo-," compares the marble collection in his right pocket with the marble collection in his left pocket, and rejoins the chorale unerringly on "ria," but neither pleading nor pummeling will induce him to vocalize all those finky "aws." All this is a little hard on Pam, who is 19 and who, as the conscientious and efficient head of her school Madrigal Club last year, has much higher standards than the rest of us. Our carol program this year was to be not just Mother at the piano, John at the recorder, and nine children singing in unison. It was to include part singing, solos, duets, trios, and quartets,

Buckley on the drums, ten-year-old Jennifer on the triangle, and a piano duet by Betsey and Alison who are 11 and 12 and hate each other.

Our first difficulties I could see coming. Buckley played the drum, not with a gently medieval boom, or even with a gay seventeenth-century ratatat, but as if he were solo-ing during a pause in a program by the Rolling Stones, which was impressive to be sure, but reduced the singers to utter inaudibility. Jennifer ting'd on the triangle whenever it seemed to her that she had not sung for quite long enough, and Betsey and Alison, who have never entirely grasped the purpose of a duet, exchanged sidelong black-eyed glares and raced each other through "Jingle Bells," Alison winning handily by a good two and a half measures.

Timothy and little Janet, who were to solo as friendly beasts in the carol known only to the parents of small children, "The Friendly Beasts," were less than cooperative. Janet refused to sing, "I, said the cow all white and red," because she said cows were ugly and she was not; besides, everyone kept smiling at her; and Tim persisted in singing, "I. Said the donkey. All Shaggy. And brown. I carried. His Mother. Uphill. And down."

After the special-effects numbers the group launched into the standard Christmas carols while Pam conducted and I concentrated on the piano. I have to concentrate harder than most people on the piano because of an abnormal tendency to play everything in D Major. Our repertoire was nearly finished when Pam addressed the group in less than a friendly tone.

"If anybody's being funny around here, they can just stop it right now."

There was a blank silence. Long blue eyes met wide black eyes without the glimmer of a twinkle. Pam waited a minute, then she said:

"Mother, let's start over, and I'll take the piano while you come out here and listen. There's something peculiar going on. Now listen *carefully*."

I listened carefully, and it was then I decided my children are either not quite bright enough to live, or else they are too gay to bear.

Do you know what "afforient" is? Neither did I till I heard Priscilla, who is 15 and who should know better, sweetly warble that she three kings afforient were, and I asked her. "Afforient," if you are interested, is the state of being disoriented, or wandering, as one does over field and fountain, moor and mountain.

And has anybody ever wondered where the Ranger is on Christmas Eve? Has anyone, for that matter, ever given a single thought to the Ranger on Christmas Eve? Well, Betsey Heath has. "*Away* is the Ranger," she will inform you, if you listen carefully. And obviously, he is away because there is no crib for his bed. After all, why should the Ranger stick around *here*, when he hasn't even got a crib much less a bed for Pete's sake!

Janet, canny little Janet, all of whose sins are premeditated and blatant, sang exactly what she intended to sing. "*No L, No L the angels did say*." It was a matter of the angels' alphabet, she explained to me a little tiredly. "A B C D E F G H I J K M N O P Q R S T U V W X Y Z. No L, get it, Mother, No L!" I eyed her suspiciously, because more humor in the family we do not need, but I let it pass.

Jennifer settled my next problem, which had to do with the angels. Do you know how the angel of the Lord shone around? He shone around in a glowy manner, that's how. While shepherds watch'd their flock by night, she explained, the angel of the Lord came and glowy showed around. How else?

Have you ever wondered, in the long watches of the night, what Child is this who laid to rest on Mary's lap is sleeping? Well, it is the child whom angels greet with Ann the Sweet, while shepherds' watches keeping. Well, St. Ann was Mary's mother, certainly sweet and probably dead, argued Alison. Why *wouldn't* she be with the angels? As for the shepherds, what with their setting off for Bethlehem, well known for its good and bad thieves, keeping their watches was a very friendly gesture on the part of the angels. Ann the Sweet probably thought of it.

Some of them were taking an individual called "Good Heed" to the angels' ward; many of them with the jellied toast proc' claiming, though all of them sang the Coventry Carol, twenty of whose 28 words are "Lully, lully," absolutely correctly.

If anyone is interested in the geography of Bethlehem, I can tell you categorically that it lies on seashore, just below the town of Dul. We know it is *below* Dul because the carol states very clearly that Bethlehem is what in Dul you see *below* (sometimes written *in dulci jubilo*) and we know it is on the sea because among the deep in dreamless sleep the silent stars go by, so that had to be the stars' *reflection*, see, Mother? Because they couldn't very well *shine* among the deep, could they, Mother?

This is the kind of thing that happens when your children get B2 in Reasoning Ability and C4 in Independent Reading.

The older children, to give credit where credit is due, made their misinterpretations on a far loftier level. Leaving history and geography to their younger siblings, Pam and Jim simply revised the Christian religion.

Pam, even Pam, kept announcing in her clear, sweet contralto that God and sin are reconciled; but she realized immediately, when it was pointed out to her, that God was far more likely to reconcile Himself to sinners than to sin, even if the book hadn't said so, which it had.

Jim had to argue a little. He was the one who kept urging the shepherds to leave their "you's" and leave their "am's" and rise up, shepherds, and follow.

"What in Heaven's name is that about you's and am's?" I asked him.

"Oh-h-h, rejection of personality, denial of self," said Jim grandly. "Practically the central thesis of Christian theology."

"Of course, I don't go to a Catholic college, but I think that's Communist theory, not Christian theology," I told him. "In any case, could you come down from those philosophic heights and join us shepherds down here with our ewes (female sheep) and rams (male sheep)."

"If you insist," said Jim, with the impudent grin of the 21-year-old whose dear mother is incontrovertibly in the right, and besides, it's right down there in black and white.

But I was too weary to go on. "Children," I said. "Let's just do one song absolutely *perfectly*. Let's concentrate on 'Silent Night,' because that's the one we know best anyway. Pam and Priscilla can do the alto, John can do the descant, the rest of you sing nice and softly and, Buckley, I don't want to hear one *note* below middle C."

They lined up, looking very clean and handsome and holy, Jim and John at the back, Timothy and Janet on either side of Pam at the piano, and the middle echelon sensibly and un-quarrelsomely distributed in the middle according to heights. *Just like the Trapp Family*, I thought to myself happily. Pam turned and gave them all a long and, I hoped, stern look, before she played the opening measures.

"*Silent night, holy night*," nine young voices chanted softly, and I noticed Jennifer and Betsey beginning to break up in twinkles and dimples. "*All is calm, all is bright*," they went on, John's recorder piping low and clear. Buckley and Alison clapped their hands briefly over their mouths. "*Round John Virgin, Mother and Child*," the chorus swelled sweetly, and I rapped hard on the piano. "Just *who*," I asked, in my most restrained voice, "is Round John Virgin?"

"One of the twelve opossums," the ten young voices answered

promptly, and they collapsed over the piano, from the piano bench onto the floor, convulsed by their own delicate wit.

And that's why we didn't have *this* year's Christmas carol program.

Afterword

"For her," an august and worldly professor of the social sciences called in when the word leaked out that she was in coma, "I have to confess I have said a prayer, for the first time in many years even though I never met her." His prayer, and others, were unavailing. Aloïse Buckley Heath died on Monday, January 16, 1967, ten days after an unsuccessful operation which was performed a few hours after she had complained of a bad headache, and was driven, by her husband, to the hospital in Hartford. Unconsciousness and partial paralysis gradually set in, and when the doctor did operate it was only because, as he put it, he would have done so on his own wife under similar circumstances—he gave her only one or two chances out of one hundred. And then a few minutes later when he actually observed the damage done by the cerebral hemorrhage, he simply stitched her back together and waited, as the family did— her husband, her ten children, her mother, her eight brothers and sisters—for the inevitable end. It came later than the young doctors had predicted. "They don't realize," said one doctor, "that at forty-eight the heart is strong. It goes right on beating, for a while, a good while. What happened to her brain is the kind of thing that usually happens to people in their late sixties or seventies. That's why she isn't dead—yet. But there won't be any pain, any consciousness." She was buried at St. Bernard's Cemetery, in Sharon, Connecticut, on Wednesday, January 18, alongside two of her sisters, who had died at age three days, and 31 years. At the service, said as she would have wanted, in Latin, a memorial card was distributed, a small photograph, the dates of birth and death on one side, and on the other a passage from François Mauriac's *Ce Que Je Crois* that she had seen and expressed admiration for—as a young girl she had been schooled in France, and she knew the language as a native—only a month before. Mauriac wrote: "*Faites, Mon Dieu, que je me recuille dans la paix de votre présence, afin que quand mon heure sera venue, je passe par une transition presque insensible, de vous à vous, de vous, pain vivant, pain des hommes, à vous amour vivant déjà possédé par ceux de mes biens-aimés qui se sont endormis avant moi dans votre amour.*"—"Grant, O Lord, that I might commune in the peace of your presence, so that when my hour is come, I shall pass through a transition all but insensible, from You to You; from You, the Living Bread, the Bread of Man, to You, the Living Love, already possessed by those of my beloved ones who, in that love, have gone before me to sleep."

"Though I never met her," one reader wrote, "I felt along with thousands of *National Review* readers, I'm sure, the force of her personality; her vibrant, joyous spirit sang out of her seasonal articles for *National Review*." "Of all the writers on your magazine, over the past 11 years," an attorney wrote, "she must surely have been the most lovable." And from a minister: "My wife, my children, and I feel something of a personal loss in the death. . . . As she has on several occasions in the past, she added to the joy of our Christmas celebration with her most recent article, [giving us] that sense of thankful and light-hearted appreciation of the mercies of God which we are trying to nurture in those whom He has given us to love."

Aloïse Heath wrote for the very first issue of *National Review*, and she had an article in the issue that was on the stands when she took sick. She did not, however, write frequently.

There was of course the handicap of her motherhood of ten children, and the very special care she took of them. Besides that she was notoriously disorganized, so much so that gener-ations of editors clamored, unsuccessfully, for her articles, and when she died, she had on her desk, as usual unanswered, a letter from the editor of a prominent monthly, begging for her copy. She had excited, at Smith College, the admiring attention of the academicians, as sharply distinguished from the admin-istrators who at one point got so fed up with her dilatory habits as to suspend her for a year (she graduated with the class of 1941, instead of 1940)—a lever against her which unfortunately no editor inherited. But the professors gave her all the ritual honors of a very bright young writer. She was married in 1942 and got around to writing an article about her first child five years later. It was published in the *Ladies' Home Journal*, and with her check for $500 she bought expensive presents for all her brothers and sisters, resolved to write regularly, and didn't; not even when the agent for Somerset Maugham—who thus announced himself—offered to handle her material. She was always acquiescent; she would agree to write anything in the world any editor asked her to write; and simply did not do so—she was too busy with her growing family. She did produce a piece for *NR* at Christmastime, the ordeal of whose parturi-tion was an annual agony—bits and pieces would come in by notepaper, telegram, telephone. But they were the most applauded pieces we ever published, even though they seldom touched on politics (one reader suggested we get Aloïse Heath to write *all* of *every* issue). Seldom, but not never . . .

Her strength was the children she loved—to the extent, she always made clear, that that was possible for anyone who truly understands children. One time she received a letter from an irrepressibly attractive and utterly impossible 13-year-old boy, friend of one of her sons, asking her whether she would recom-mend him to a school into which he sought admittance. (The entire, hilarious correspondence caught the eye of the *Reader's Digest*, which published it in its entirety.)

She knew children, and knew the duty of the parent to try to dominate children, but knew also the limits of any such ambition, children being—children. "If they start throwing books at each other," she wrote in a piece about carpools, "it is best to park the car on the side of the road and exhibit emotional stability until they've stopped. Even this is unnecessary if the books are being thrown by Fourth, Fifth, or Sixth Form boys. Their aim is invariably excellent, and you are in no danger whatsoever."

Always she insisted on the realisms. There was the Christmas when she announced to her children that they would attempt a Trapp Family Christmas, the distinguishing feature of which was that each child would select another child (by ballot) as his special protégé (*Christkindl*), and proceed to shower (anonymously) special favors upon him or her until Christmas Day when the *Christkindl*'s benefactor would identify himself. The idea was heroically launched. But her children didn't appear to be exactly Trapp-minded . . .

"I didn't see how the *Christkindl* custom could go wrong, though. I *still* don't. In the Trapp family, everyone writes his name on a piece of paper and the papers are put in a basket which is passed around as soon as the children have finished singing: 'Ye heavens, dew drop from above.' Everybody picks a name from the basket, and the pickee, if you follow me, becomes the picker's secret *Christkindl*, and the idea is, you do your *Christkindl* a good turn every day until Christmas without ever letting him know who you are . . ." But at her house it was, as usual, chaotic . . . the children found themselves picking themselves, or prematurely divulging their identities, or whatever. Finally, she contrived a means by which the children would pick out their *Christkindl*, and be picked out. It was not altogether democratic, and by no means left to chance. She